AF256000

Middleton Family History

by Karen Proudler & Pauline Batty

First Published in Great Britain in 2013
by Karen & Graham Proudler
Forge Cottage, Field Farm, Aston Lane, Shardlow
Derbys DE72 2GX

Copyright © 2013 Karen Proudler
All rights reserved.
The right of Karen Proudler and Pauline Batty to be identified
as Authors of this work has been asserted by them in accordance
with the Copyright, Designs and Patent Act 1988.

A CIP catalogue record for this book is
available from the British Library.

ISBN: 978-0-9566831-2-0

No part of this book may be reproduced or transmitted in any form or by any means, electronic or mechanical including photocopying, recording or by any information storage and retrieval system, without permission from the Publisher in writing. No guarantee is made or implied that the information contained herein is without error. Information is for readers' convenience and reference only, anyone requiring accurate information should verify same by seeking professional assistance and conducting their own further research.

All dates prior to 1752 are old style unless stated otherwise

CONTENTS

INTRODUCTION

This booklet is an examination of one branch of Middletons from Yorkshire. From first beginnings in idyllic rural Wensleydale in North Yorkshire, we follow the family chronologically through the centuries to the twentieth century where descendants are spread far and wide. Theirs is a story of the changing times: from the earliest days where they are farming, through the upheaval of land enclosure when they become farm workers or engaged in cottage industries, to relocation to the towns and cities as the process of industrialisation draws them to the heavy industries and town living in Durham.

This research was undertaken as part of a family history study of Edith Annie Middleton 1899-1972 where we mapped out both her ancestors and descendants.

Author Pauline Batty is a grand-daughter, and Karen's husband Graham Proudler is a grandson of Edith Middleton.

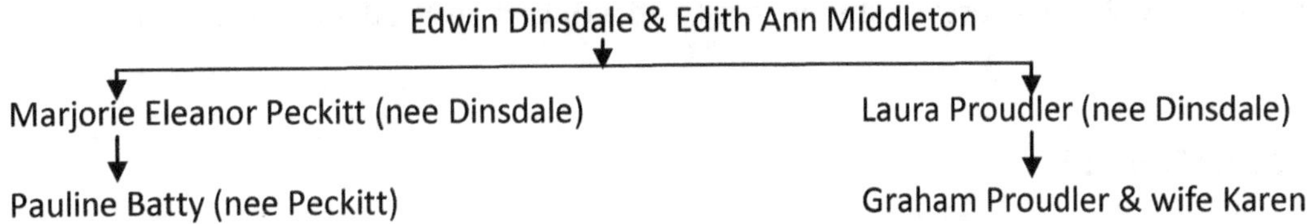

Acknowledgements

This book has been compiled from a variety of sources, including public records and, most importantly, the input of family members with most branches of the family being consulted. Both authors wish to thank everyone who has contributed with photographs, stories and information that has enabled us to piece the family history together.

Frequency of the name

	1881	2012	Change
Middleton	15,722	20,572	Slight decrease in percentage of population[1]

Frequency of name in 1881 was 525 per million population
Current frequency of name is 448 per million.

Origin of the name

Likely to be derived from a place name, although there were over twenty place names called Middleton in England so it is possible for numerous unconnected branches to have arisen. As surnames were required to identify people moving around the country, many took their birth village/town as a surname. The literal translation of Middleton is "middle town" or "farmstead".

One of the earliest records shows a Robert de Mideltone in 1166 Eynsham Chartulary, Oxfordshire, then a William de Midelton in 1327 (from Sussex Subsidy Rolls)[2] and a Gilbert de Middelton in 1273.

Family movements

Generation 1	1734-1762 Aysgarth/Carperby	1762-1775 Low Burton/Well/Snape area	
Generation 2	1736-1762 Aysgarth/Carperby	1762-1811 Low Burton/Well/Snape area	
Generation 3	1780-1803 Low Burton/Well/Snape area	1806-1861 South of Catterick: Killerby/Bedale Hornby/Ainderby Myers	
Generation 4	1810-1841 South of Catterick: Killerby/ Great Fencote, Kirkby Fleetham)	1844-1876, 1901 Middleton Tyas	
Generation 5	1845-1881 Middleton Tyas	1881-1886 Richmond: Dalton & Croft-on-Tees	
Generation 6	1867-1894 Middleton Tyas	1894-1905 Cotherstone	1905-1941 Darlington
Generation 7	1899-1905 Cotherstone	1905-1972 Darlington	
Generation 8+	Darlington and beyond		

---

[1] www.britishsurnames.co.uk
[2] Oxford's Dictionary of English Surnames by R.M. Wilson

MIDDLETON FAMILY TREE

1st generation
John MIDDLETON circa 1703-1787
Married Joan Forster at Aysgarth

2nd generation
John MIDDLETON 1736-1811
Married Ann Robinson at Aysgarth

3rd generation
Mark MIDDLETON 1779-1837 of Well
Married Jane Lockey

4th generation
Thomas MIDDLETON 1812-1876, Killerby Nr Catterick
Married Hannah

5th generation
Hannah MIDDLETON 1845-1886, Middleton Tyas
Married (later) Christopher Barker

6th generation
John Chapman MIDDLETON 1867-1941, Middleton Tyas
Married Marie Bainbridge

7th generation+
Edith Annie MIDDLETON 1899-1972, Cotherstone/Darlington
Married Edwin DINSDALE

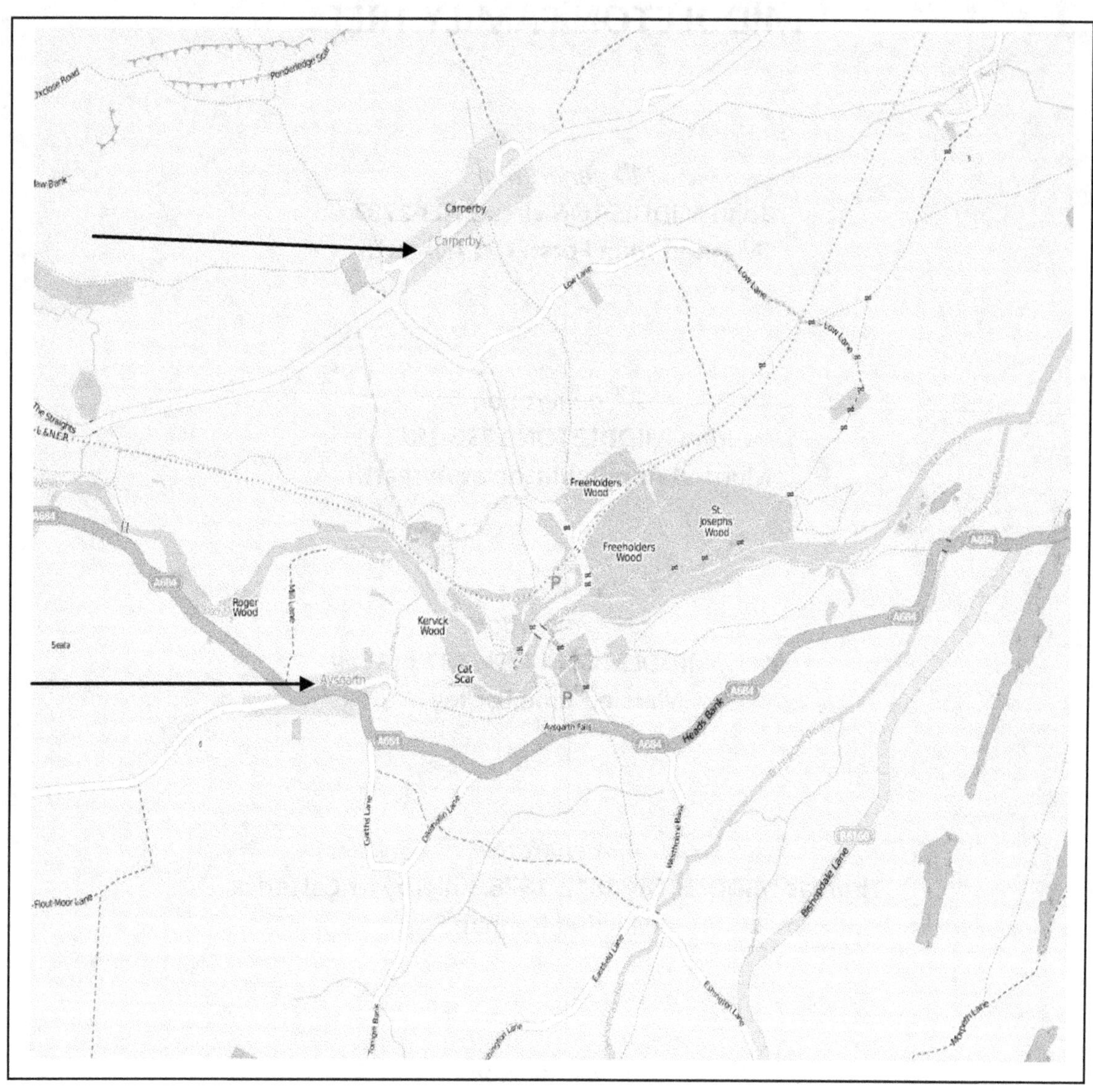

3 "© OpenStreetMap contributors".

3 http://www.openstreetmap.org/copyright

JOHN MIDDLETON - circa 1703-1787

Generation No. 1

JOHN[1] MIDDLETON was born about 1703 in Durham and was buried on 23rd March 1787 at St Michael's in Well, Yorkshire. He married JOAN FORSTER on 4th February 1734 at St Andrew's Church in Aysgarth, Yorkshire. She was born about 1710 in Carperby, Yorkshire, and was buried on 25 March 1774 at St Mary's Church at Masham.

Children of JOHN MIDDLETON and JOAN FOSTER are:

    i.   JOHN MIDDLETON, b. September 5, 1736, Aysgarth
    ii.   WILLIAM MIDDLETON, b. 1738 Aysgarth
    iii.   ELIZABETH MIDDLETON, b. 1740 Aysgarth
    iv.   ISABELLA MIDDLETON, b. September 4, 1743, Aysgarth
    v.   ANN MIDDLETON, baptised 10 Mar 1748 Aysgarth
    vi.   JANE MIDDLETON, b. 1754 Aysgarth

Our first Middleton ancestor's precise origins are a mystery. We can estimate his birth date to be around 1703 and, from his marriage record below, we know he came from Durham, but since Durham is both a City and a County name there is no way to be certain of his whereabouts before marriage.

There is, however, a marriage of a John Middleton on 7th June 1703 at St Giles Church in Durham, followed by the birth of a son John who was baptised on 21st November in 1703. The parish register entry says:

"21 November 1703 Baptism of John, son of John Middleton, a Traveller, a Stranger"

But, even if we did find evidence that this was our John Middleton, his father being a traveller and stranger to the parish would still leave the trail cold unfortunately.

John marries in Aysgarth to Joan Forster in 1734 but scrutiny of the Aysgarth parish registers shows no Middletons in that parish before this marriage, though there are numerous Forsters. The marriage record in the original parish register is too faint to reproduce here, so this is a transcription....

Marriage Record

> Marriage on 4th Feb 1734 at St Andrew's Church, Aysgarth
>
> John Middleton of Durham and
>
> Joan Forster of Carperby - By Publication

The original entry in the parish register was found by Sheila Middleton of Australia. Sheila is a distant relation, via Jane Middleton - third child of John Middleton (generation number 2).

The six children born to John and Joan have their births recorded in Aysgarth but it is thought that the family probably lived in nearby Carperby which did not have its own parish church and so used St Andrew's Church, Aysgarth.

Children of John and Joan Middleton

John	William	Elizabeth	Isabella	Ann	Jane
1736-1811	1738-1806	1740-aft 1775	1743	1749	1754
b.Aysgarth d. Well	b. Aysgarth d. Askrigg	b.Aysgarth	b. Aysgarth	b. Aysgarth	b.Aysgarth

From their marriage in 1734 through to the early 1760s, this family are resident in this area.

Quakerism

It is possible that Carperby's[4] reputation as a centre for Quakerism drew John Middleton there. The following article, by Helen E Roberts for the Yorkshire Quaker Heritage Project explains:-

> "The first reference to Quaker activity in this area is to the preaching of Richard Robinson in Carperby around 1658/9. The reaction was mainly one of hostility and it was several years before he preached there again, this time with more success. A number of families were convinced and joined neighbouring Coverdale Meeting. The Conventicle Act of 1670 unleashed a wave of persecution in the Yorkshire Dales, due largely to the work of an informer, William Thornaby of Richmond. At this point, the local centre of Quaker worship was the home of Thomas Simpson at West Burton in Bishopdale. Meetings were broken up on a regular basis and Friends were fined a total of £450 over a 14-month period. In 1689 there were six meeting places registered in the parish of Aysgarth (in Carperby and West Burton), but a Meeting House did not open in Aysgarth itself until 1704, situated in a converted barn behind Constable House. For many years, this was also home to Richmond Monthly Meeting. A Meeting House was acquired in Carperby in the same year. From about 1790 until its closure c.1802, Langstrothdale Meeting was closely allied with Aysgarth."[5]

It is also interesting that the leader of the Quakers in Carperby at that time was a Richard Robinson because, John Middleton's eldest son - also called John 1736-1811 was to marry an Ann Robinson from Aysgarth. It is not known if there was a Robinson family connection.

Move to Low Burton/Snape/Well area

Around 1760, eldest son John leaves the area to work at Highfield Farm in Well (Bedale). John returns to Aysgarth in 1762 to marry his already pregnant future wife Ann Robinson. It is at this time that most of the family make the move eastwards, probably only a distance of some twenty miles - and relocate in the area of Well/Little Burton - close to where son John is working. It is thought that most of the family move to that area. Eldest son John will head up our second generation.

---

[4] From The Yorkshire Dales: North and East - Swaledale, Wensleydale, volume 2
[5] Researching Yorkshire Quaker History - A Guide to Sources, compiled by Helen E Roberts for the Yorkshire Quaker Heritage Project. Published by The University of Hull, Brynmor Jones Library, 2003 (updated 2007).

Some records have been found which show at least two locations for family members - close by each other; the parents in Low Burton near Masham and son John at Highfield Farm near Snape. The death record, in 1774, of John's wife Joan says .... "Burial of Joan Middleton on 25th March 1774 at St Mary's, Masham, Yorkshire, wife of John Middleton of Low Burton". So Low Burton seems to be where the parents were living.

Low Burton

Low Burton is within walking distance of Masham, being just across the River Ure, which is crossed by Masham Bridge, built in 1754 (which replaced an ancient bridge). It had few residents, though historically it may have been of more significance as it has been described as 'an ancient residence around which are indications of moat and earthworks'.[6] In 'The History and Antiquities of Masham' John Fisher describes Burton as being, formerly, a village belonging to the township of Well but that it had become a distinct manor. Writing, in 1865, he said that 'Little Burton, or Low Burton estate is another manor, of which G.J. Yarburgh Esq of Heslington Hall near York is the Lord'.[7]

John may have been employed as an agricultural labourer there perhaps minding the horned cattle or sheep - which was the dominant employment at the time[8].

Burial of Joan

John dies within one year of his wife Joan and is buried at St Michael's in Well.[9]

Burial of Joan Middleton

on 25 March 1774

at St Mary's, Masham, Yorkshire

wife of John Middleton of Low Burton

Burial of John

John is survives his wife by 13 years and it is thought the burial in 1787 at St Michael's Church in Well is his. No gravestone for either John or Joan has been found.

Burial of John Middleton on 23 March 1787

at St Michael's, Well

---

[6] Wensleydale and the Lower Vale of the Lore from Ouseburn to Lunds Fell by Edmund Bogg.

[7] "Burton, it will be seen, was formerly a berewick or village, belonging to the township of Well. The township of Burton-upon-Yore, although situate within the parish of Masham, does not form any part of Mashamshire. It consists now of three distinct manors: the Aldborough estate, together with the Greens and Nutwith Cote, are parcel of the manor of Aldborough Grange, of which John T.D. Hutton Esq is the Lord. The Little Burton, or Low Burton estate is another manor, of which G.J. Yarburhg Esq of Heslington Hall near York is the Lord and Great or High Burton, as it is now called, is another manor of which James Pullelne esq of Clifton Castle is the Lord".

[8] From: 'Parishes: Masham', A History of the County of York North Riding: Volume 1 (1914), pp. 323-332. URL: http://www.british-history.ac.uk/report.aspx?compid=64761 Date accessed: 01 April 2013.

[9] National Burial Index, Cleveland Family History Society

Masham   **Low Burton**   **Well**[10]   **Snape**

"© OpenStreetMap contributors".

---

[10] http://www.openstreetmap.org/copyright

JOHN MIDDLETON - 1736-1811

Generation No. 2

JOHN[2] MIDDLETON *(JOHN[1])* was baptised September 5, 1736 in Aysgarth, Yorkshire, and died 1811 in Well, Yorkshire. He married ANN ROBINSON. She was born 1740 in Aysgarth, Yorkshire, and died 1796 in Well.

Children of JOHN MIDDLETON and ANN ROBINSON are:
    i.   JOHN MIDDLETON, b.1762, Aysgarth
    ii.   ANN MIDDLETON, b. 1765, Well.
    iii.   THOMAS MIDDLETON, b. 1767, Well
    iv.   WILLIAM MIDDLETON b. 1770, Well
    v.   JANE MIDDLETON, b. 1773, Well
    vi.   HENRY MIDDLETON, b. 1776.
    vii.   ELIZABETH MIDDLETON bap 1776, Well
    viii.   CHRIS MIDDLETON ? d. 1777, Well
    ix.   MARK MIDDLETON, b. April 30, 1780, Well

Baptism Record

John Middleton is baptised 5 September 1736 in Aysgarth, Yorkshire at St Andrew's Church. He marries Ann Robinson (1740-1796) when he is 26 years old and she is 22. It was a 'shotgun' wedding, with wife Ann already pregnant by the time they marry in July of 1762 and their first child is baptised in November of that year. John must have already have been spending time away from Aysgarth - for his employment as a farm worker, because at their wedding he was said to be "of High Field in the parish of Well" (that is High Field House).

Highfield House Farm, where John was working, still exists today (see map on the next page for location). It was just off Watlass Lane - which is west of Snape/Well. If you travel along Watlass Lane, in the direction of Snape, you will see on the right is Moor Lane and we have one note (unsourced) which claims that John and Ann's address at the time was Moor End Lane which, depending exactly where they were on Moor Lane, would have placed them close to his place of employment.

Transcript of the original parish record entry (which is too feint to reproduce) at St Andrew's Aysgarth, Yorkshire says:-

    "John Middleton of High Field in ye parish of Well and Ann Robinson of Carperby were married by licence July 1st, 1762".

Marriage of John Middleton and Ann Robinson

on 1st July 1762

at St Andrew's Aysgarth

A map of the area identifies the location of Highfield House Farm[11]:

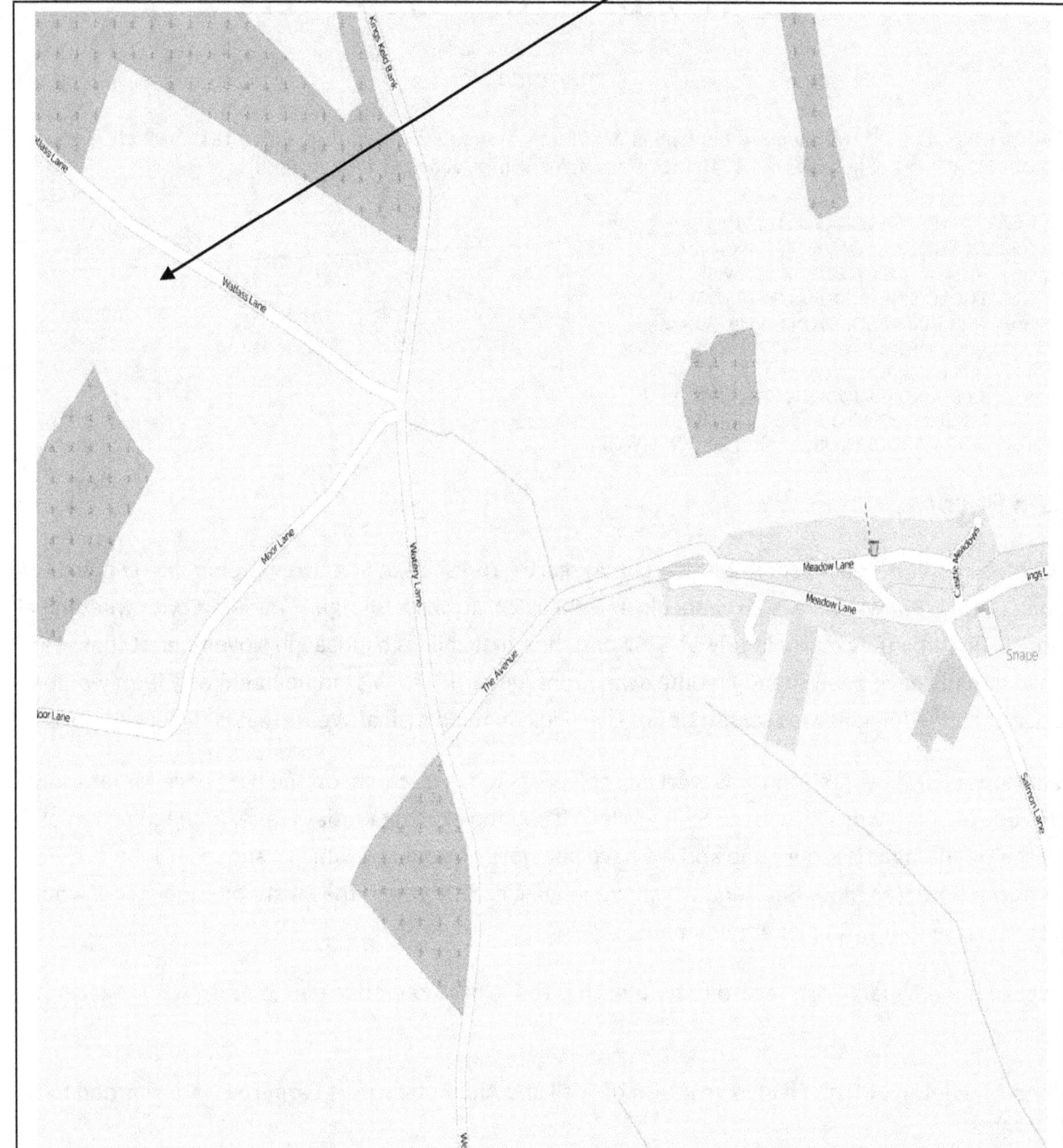

"© OpenStreetMap contributors".

John and Ann's first born child was registered in Aysgarth, but thereafter the others are all at Snape/Well - which is the nearest village to Highfield House Farm.   They spend the rest of their lives living here, having some nine children, but not all survive.

---

[11] http://www.openstreetmap.org/copyright

Children of John and Ann

John	Ann	Thomas	William	Jane	Chris*	Elizabeth	Henry*	Mark
1762	1765	1767	1770	1773	d.1777	1776	c. 1776	1780
Aysgarth	Well	Well	Well	Well	Well	Well	Well	Well

* No baptism records have been found for either Chris or Henry.

Ann dies at the age of 56 years[12] ....

Ann is buried on

17 April 1796 at St Michael's, Well

and John dies some 15 years later and is also buried in Well, Yks[13].

Burial of John Middleton on

10th March 1811 at St Michael's, Well

Ann Robinson

Ann was baptised on 10th April 1740 at Aysgarth. Her parents were Leonard Robinson and Ann Richardson and they were married on 15th August 1726 at West Witton, which is a short distance away from Carperby. Leonard was buried in 1794 at nearby Askrigg.

It is not known if Ann is descended from the famous Richard Robinson 1628-93 whose Quaker activities dominated the area of Aysgarth and Carperby. Richard married Margaret and had 9 children: Michael b. 1653, George b. 1655, Johnson b. 1657, Mary b. 1661, Ephraim b. 1662, Edward b. 1665, Emanual b. 1668, Rebecca b. 1672 and Rachel b. 1673 - all born in Aysgarth.

And this is the church that the Middletons, whilst at Well, would use for baptisms/marriages and burials ....

St Michael's Church, Well, is on the northern side of Church Street, at the eastern edge of the village of Well, near Bedale.

---

[12] IGI Batch numbers for Well events are: I04332-0, 1, 2, 3, 4, 5, 6, 7, 8, 9.
[13] Source: National Burial Index, Cleveland FHS. (IGI records the name as Kiddleton).

John's sister, Elizabeth, born 1740 travelled with her brother and parents to this village and married in the 1770s:-

Transcript of the original parish register entry follows:-

"Banns of marriage between Thomas Annal and Elizabeth Middleton, both of this parish, were published the 10th, 17th and 24th February 1771 by me Robt Radcliffe, curate. The said Thos Annal and Elizabeth Middleton were married in this church by banns this 25th day of February 1771 by me Jn. Baines - Minister. In the presence of us Andrew Ball, William James, this marriage was solemnized between us, Thomas Annall and Elizabeth Middleton (X) her mark."

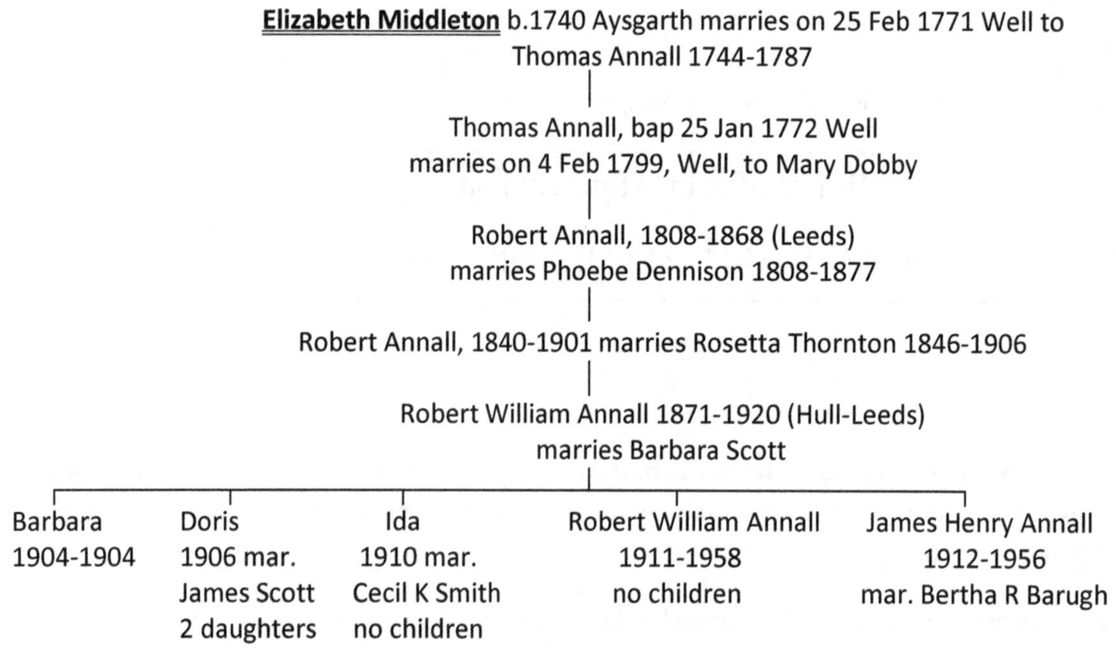

Mark Middleton - 1780-1837

Generation No. 3

MARK[3] MIDDLETON *(JOHN[2], JOHN[1])* was baptised April 30, 1780 in Well, Yorkshire, and was buried on May 28, 1837 in Catterick, York. He married JANE LOCKEY January 24, 1803. She was baptised 24 October 1777 in Snape, (daughter of Andrew Lockey) and was buried April 28, 1861 in Catterick, Yorkshire.

Children of MARK MIDDLETON and JANE LOCKEY are:
- i. MARY MIDDLETON, b. July 20, 1806, Catterick
- ii. JOHN MIDDLETON, b. 1808, Catterick
- iii. WILLIAM MIDDLETON born 1810, Catterick
- iv. THOMAS MIDDLETON, b. April 22, 1812, Catterick
- v. SARAH MIDDLETON, b. August 5, 1813, Catterick
- vi. HANNAH MIDDLETON, b. November 2, 1817, Catterick
- vii. JANE MIDDLETON, b. April 1, 1821, Catterick
- viii. ELIZABETH MIDDLETON, b. February 16, 1823, Catterick
- ix. MARGARET MIDDLETON, b. May 15, 1825, Catterick

Mark Middleton was baptised 30 April 1780 at St Michael's Church, Well in Yorkshire; he was the youngest of his family.

Baptism of Mark Middleton

on 30th April 1780

St Michael's Church, Well

At the age of 23 years, he marries Jane Lockey .....

On 24th January 1803,

Mr Mark Middleton of Well, YKS

to Jane Lockey of Gainford, Durham

(Northumberland and Durham Family History Society).

Wife Jane was born in 1775 in Gainford, Durham.

Both Mark and Jane were agricultural labourers but, beyond that, little more is known about Mark.

Children of Mark and Jane

Mark and Jane have nine children and all are baptised at Catterick - where the parents remained for the rest of their lives.

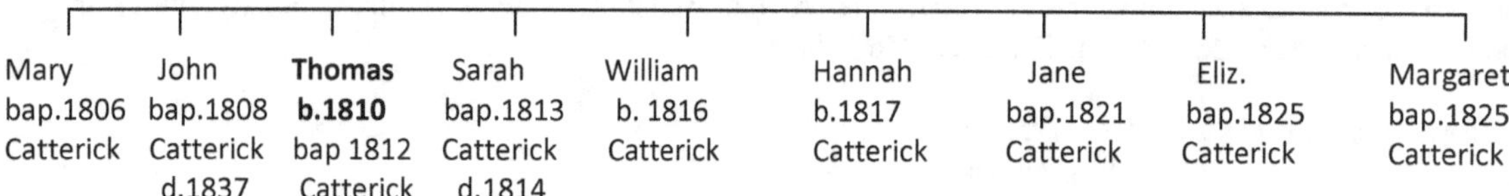

Mary	John	**Thomas**	Sarah	William	Hannah	Jane	Eliz.	Margaret
bap.1806	bap.1808	**b.1810**	bap.1813	b. 1816	b.1817	bap.1821	bap.1825	bap.1825
Catterick	Catterick	bap 1812	Catterick	Catterick	Catterick	Catterick	Catterick	Catterick
	d.1837	Catterick	d.1814					

Burial Records- Mark

Mark died at the age of 55 - see below[14].

Date of Burial : 28th May 1837

Mark Middleton

Age at death: 55 years. Place of burial (St Anne's, Catterick)

St Anne's Church, Catterick

Monumental Inscriptions have been transcribed by the Cleveland Family History Society for both St Anne's Church and surrounding graveyard and Catterick Cemetery, but no record of a headstone has been found for either Mark or his wife Jane, so it is presumed they were buried without any.

---

[14] National Burial Index; Cleveland Family History Society.

Mrs Mark Middleton

Jane outlives Mark and she is to be found on the first census return of 1841. At this time she is living with her married daughter Hannah Sugden and her family at Low Street, Killerby nr Catterick.

1841 census

Township of Killerby (Catterick) at Low Street, Jane Middleton, age 55, agricultural labourer of this county; James Sugden[15], age 20, agricultural labourer of this county; Hannah Sugden, age 20; Mark Sugden, 1 month[16]

Killerby

The above place name 'Killerby', on modern maps, is hard to find. There is 'a' Killerby located seven miles north of Darlington, but this is not the one where the Middletons lived.

One mile south of Catterick, there was an estate called 'Killerby' which was owned by the Booth family. Thomas Booth (1755-1835) was a famous cattle breeder - his sons continued breeding prime cattle after their father died. So this Killerby became known as the township of Killerby in the parish of Catterick, (wapentake of East Hang, North Riding County York). It is situated about five miles north of Bedale, near to the River Swale.

Three of Mark and Jane's children marry at St Anne's Church at Catterick[17]. First son John on 25 Nov 1837 to Frances Metcalf, secondly Jane on 9 October 1839 to Jonathan Tweddel and thirdly Hannah Middleton married James Sugden[18] on 24 October 1840.[19]

1851 census

Ten years later and Jane is still living with her daughter's family: Hannah and James Sugden have moved to Little Houses, Bedale with their growing family of son Mark, age 9, James age 8, William age 5, John age 2 and Thomas age 2 months.[20] Jane resides with them and is referred to on the 1851 census as a widowed pauper (formerly agricultural labourer) Her birth place and age are recorded incorrectly - the records say she was born at Gainforth and it was Gainford in Durham and her age is recorded as 69 when, in fact, she was 74.

1861 Census

Census day in 1861 was 7th-8th April, but Jane is not to be found on the 1861 census. She dies on 25th April 1861 and is buried on the 28th.

---

15 This surname is spelt Sugdon on the 1841 census, but subsequently Sugden.
16 Piece 1250, book/folio 16/2A, page 3.
17 IGI Batch Number M09818-1.
18 This entry on the IGI is recorded, incorrectly, as "Lugdon" instead of Sugdon/Sugden.
19 It is possible that the fourth Middleton to marry at this same church at the same time - Ann - is a daughter to Mark/Jane (rather than a niece) but evidence for this has not been found. (Ann, 4 Dec 1833 to James Flemming)
20 1851 census H0107, piece 2378, folio 5, page 2 Bedale.

Burial Record - Jane

Date of Burial : 28th April 1861

Jane Middleton

Age at death: 84 years. Place of burial (St Anne's Catterick)

Jane's death certificate has been obtained:-

REGISTRATION DISTRICT: BEDALE

1861 Death in the Sub-district of Bedale in the County of York

No. 221. When and where died: Twenty-fifth April 1861 at Holtby Cottages, Ainderby-Myers. Name: Jane Middleton. Female. Age 84 years. Occupation: widow of Mark Middleton a farm labourer. Cause of death: old age, not certified. Signature, description and residence of informant: "X" the mark of James Fleming, present at death, Holtby Cottages, Ainderby Myers. When registered:27th April 1861. Registrar: William Wade.

It is difficult to account for Jane being in Ainderby-Myers and the presence of a James Flemming at her death in 1861. She had been living with her daughter for at least 10 years, from 1841-51 and perhaps longer, then on the 1861 census she is not present with them, so it is possible that in the final few months/weeks of her life she was taken into the care of the local North Allerton Union, perhaps if she needed continual nursing care. Ainderby-Myers came under the jurisdiction of North Allerton which, following the 1837 Poor Law Union Bill[21], had been busy erecting new workhouses throughout the parish. The North Riding of Yorkshire had 35 workhouses in 1776 with a combined capacity of over 1,000. Jane was described, on the 1851 census, as a widowed pauper and it is perhaps likely that she was either interred into a workhouse for her final care or, possibly, put into some almshouses in Ainderby.

James Flemming, who was present at her death, may have been a carer or visitor on the day she died, or maybe even have been a relation. There is a marriage of an Ann Middleton to a James Flemming on 4 Dec 1833 at Catterick and James Flemming, married, is present on the 1861 census in Ainderby-Myers where he is living on the High Street.

With Ainderby Myers being such a small hamlet - a house by house search on the census return was done, but there is no reference to Holtby Cottages, where Jane dies, being included in the census at all.

---

[21] The History and Antiquities of North Allerton by Christopher John Davison Ingledew.

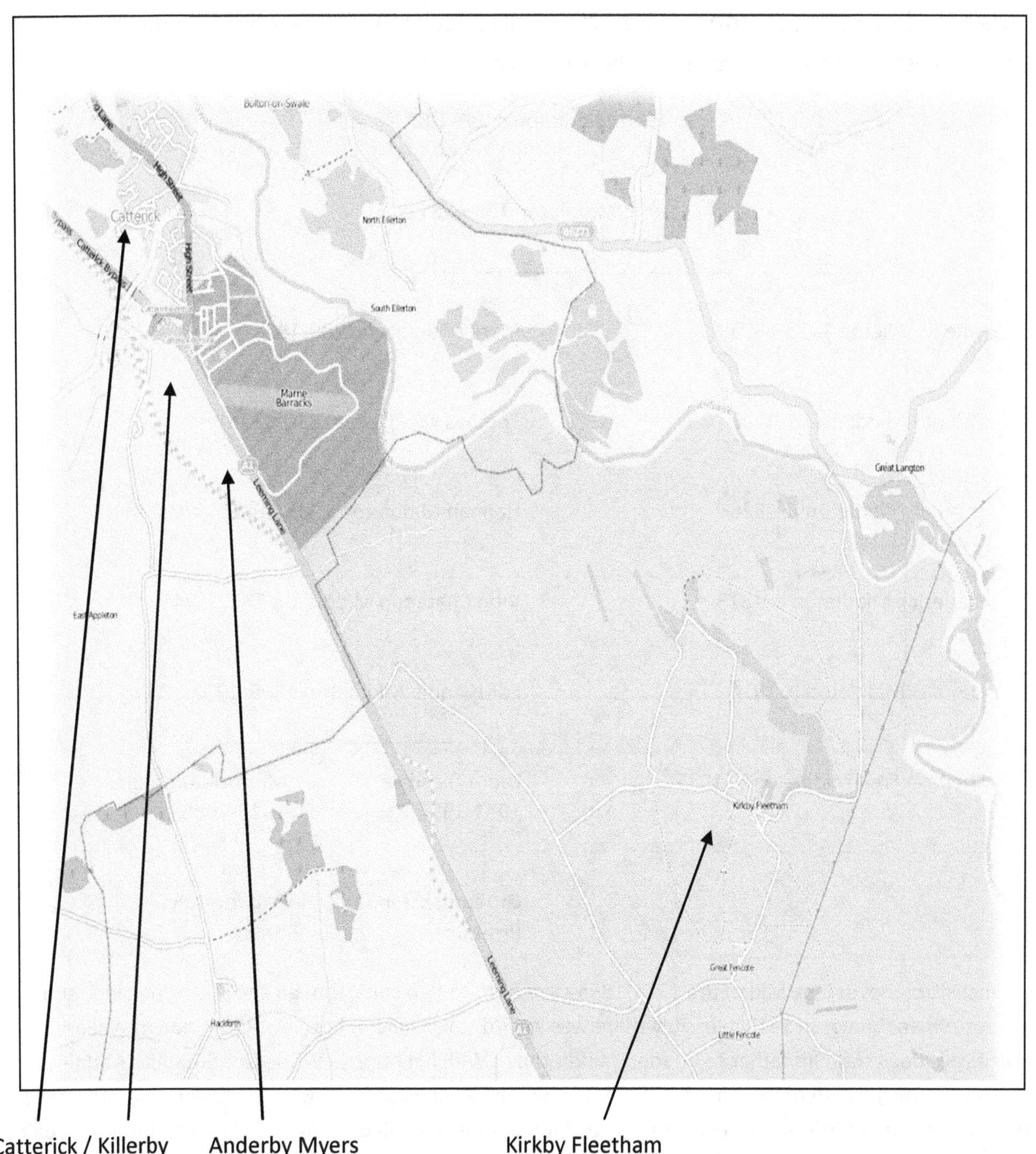

Catterick / Killerby   Anderby Myers   Kirkby Fleetham

"© OpenStreetMap contributors".[22]

---

[22] http://www.openstreetmap.org/copyright

Mark's Sister Jane 1773-1855

We have been fortunate to find another researcher whose own ancestors connect to ours …..

How the Middleton Researchers Connect: Sheila Middleton has been researching her Middleton ancestry for many years. This is how we all connect:-

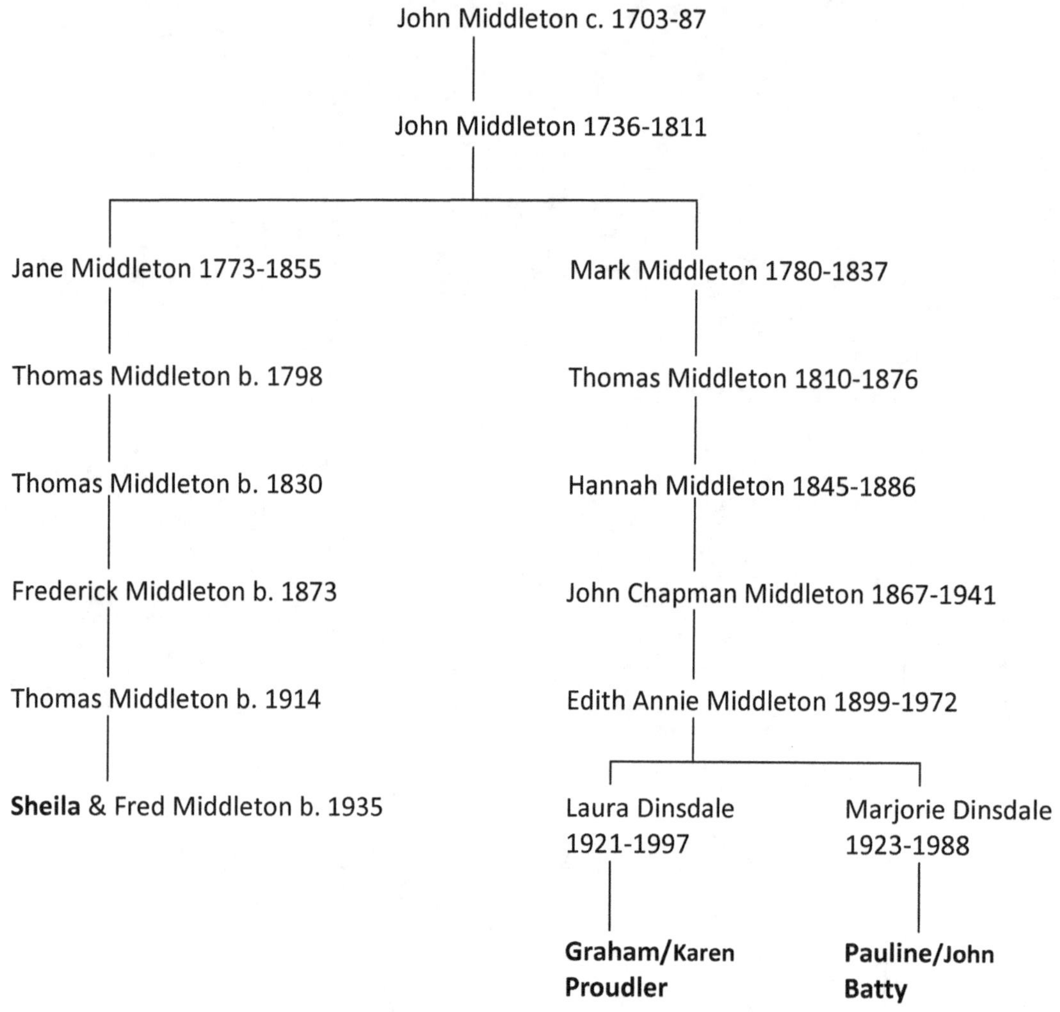

Sheila's ancestor (above) Jane Middleton 1773-1855 gave birth to two sons, though she never married: sons Thomas in 1798 and James in 1813. Possibly there was a third son, William, born in 1799 - though William's birth certificate does state his father to be John Middleton of Well (labourer). Witnesses Elizabeth Middleton (perhaps his mother) and George Dobson. This would be John Middleton (b. 1762) - 3rd generation. The 1851 census, however, shows William (whose 'birth certificate' parents had died) living at Phlashett Street in Bedale - living with a son called William b. 1837 - from William Senior's first marriage - but also residing with the family is the mother Jane (b. 1775 unmarried). So, although the official records indicate his parents to be John b. 1762 and Elizabeth - it is possible that unmarried Jane b. 1775 was his real mother.

Jane must have been in need of parish relief as Sheila found the following in the records from about the year 1823 ….. "That Jane Middleton's boys be allowed a pare [sic] of shoes. Ordered that Jane Middleton to be allowed two shillings per week on condition she sends her boys out to work at Mr Matt Mood's or to sum [sic] other person."   Matthew Mood 1778-1851, on the 1841 census, is listed as being resident at Park Street in Masham, occupation farmer.

Then in 1825 there is a further entry ..."A necessary and humane solution! Agreed that James Middleton, son of Jane Middleton, be clothed, as he is going into service".[23]

Son James was present at the death of his mother, Jane, on 1st Feb 1855 in Well. The death certificate states:

> Registration in Bedale, death in Masham, County of York. Entry #384
> Died 1st February 1855 - Well - Jane Middleton - female 86 years.
> Domestic Servant. Cause of death old age, not certified.
> Informant James Middleton, present at death, Woolcomber of Well.
> Registered 2nd February 1855. Registrar George Jackson.

By the time of the first census in 1841 James is living in Church Street (right next to St Michael's), married to wife Jane and is employed as a woolcomber in Well. He marries, has a large family and dies in 1890 and remains in Well throughout that time. The area of Snape/Well had developed wool-combing as a cottage industry which peaked in the year 1823 and the population of Snape increased to 689 at the time. This practice, however, sharply declined when the industry was industrialized[24] with the establishment of large woollen mills soon after[25].

Also on the 1841 census and living a few doors away from James in Church Street is his mother Jane who is living in a household with a widowed Elizabeth Middleton (sister-in-law) and two orphans - Mary Ann and Mark Binks - grandchildren of Jane's sister Ann 1765-1837.

Jane's other son Thomas, born 1798, marries firstly to an Elizabeth Sickling, who dies after having one child; he then marries a Mary Sickling (niece of Elizabeth) and they move to Sharow in Ripon and have a large family.

> *Transcript:* Entry for St Michael's Church in Well. Thomas Middleton of this Parish and
> Elizabeth Sickling of this Parish were married in this Church by Banns with Consent this
> Twenty First Day of May in the Year One Thousand Eight Hundred and Twenty One by me
> Thomas Dockery Vicar. Both sign with their X marks.

> *Transcript:* Thomas Middleton of this Parish and Mary Sickling of this Parish were married in
> this Church by Banns this third day of November in the Year One Thousand Eight Hundred
> Twenty Seven by me Thomas Dockeray Vicar. This Marriage was solemnized between us
> Tho. Middleton, X, his mark and Mary Sickling, her X mark, in the presence of Edmund
> Burton, his X mark and Isabella Sickling, her X mark.

---

[23] Well and Snape Parochial Records.
[24] Local aristocrat, Samuel Cunliffe Lister, 1st Baron Masham 1815-1906, who lived at Swinton Park, near Masham, invented the device that was to mechanise wool-combing.
[25] Snape Local History Group.

THOMAS MIDDLETON 1810-1876

Generation No. 4

THOMAS[4] MIDDLETON *(MARK[3], JOHN[2], JOHN[1])* was born in April 1810 and baptised April 22, 1812 in Killerby, nr Catterick, Yorkshire, and died 1876. He married HANNAH AYTON. She was baptised on 13 July 1820 in Brompton-by-Northallerton,Yorkshire, and died in 1900 Richmond. THOMAS MIDDLETON: Occupation: Labourer. Address on 1871 census: 43 Middleton Tyas HANNAH: At The Rookery with grandchildren John Chapman and Louisa on 1891 census.

Children of THOMAS MIDDLETON and HANNAH are:

    i.   MARK[5] MIDDLETON, b. 1838, Hang East, Hornby Castle.
    ii.   JOHN MIDDLETON, b. 1839; d. Bef. 1851.
    iii.   THOMAS MIDDLETON, b. 1840, Kirkby Fleetham.
    iv.   HANNAH MIDDLETON, b. May 1845, Middleton Tyas
    v.   WILLIAM MIDDLETON, b. 1846, Middleton Tyas
    vi.   JANE MIDDLETON, b. October 28, 1849, Middleton Tyas
    vii.   MARY ANNE MIDDLETON, b. November 30, 1851.
    viii.   ELIZABETH MIDDLETON, b. June 11, 1854, Middleton Tyas
    ix.   ALICE MIDDLETON, b. January 28, 1857, Middleton Tyas
    x.   EMILY MIDDLETON, b. October 13, 1861.
    xi.   ELIZA MIDDLETON, b. August 30, 1863.
    xii.   ISABELLA MIDDLETON, b. November 9, 1865.

Rrecords indicate that Thomas was baptised in 1812 at Killerby (near Catterick) which is 10 miles south of Middleton Tyas, York, though his age recorded on census returns later suggests his birth was around 1810.

> ### 1812
> ### Baptism of Thomas Middleton on 28th April at Catterick, York (son of Mark and Jane)

Although no marriage record has been found[26] we know from census returns (and their daughter Hannah's birth certificate in 1845) that he married Hannah Ayton from Brompton-by-Northallerton around 1837, just before civil records began and that they had a large family. This is Thomas with his new growing family on the 1841 census:

> ## Township of Kirkby Fleetham
> ## Address: Great Fencote
> ## Thomas Middleton, age 25 - agricultural labourer, of this county
> ## Hannah Middleton, age 20 - of this county
> ## Mark Middleton, age 3 - of this county
> ## John Middleton, age 2 - of this county
> ## Thomas Middleton, age 14 weeks, of this county
> ## Christiana Ayton, age 20, of this county

Ages, as usual on the 1841 census, rounded up or down to the nearest five years.

---

[26] There was a Wesleyan Chapel at Patrick Brompton-by-Northallerton as early as 1829 and so a search of those records may reveal the marriage entry and baptism of their first two children.

Wife Hannah Ayton's family

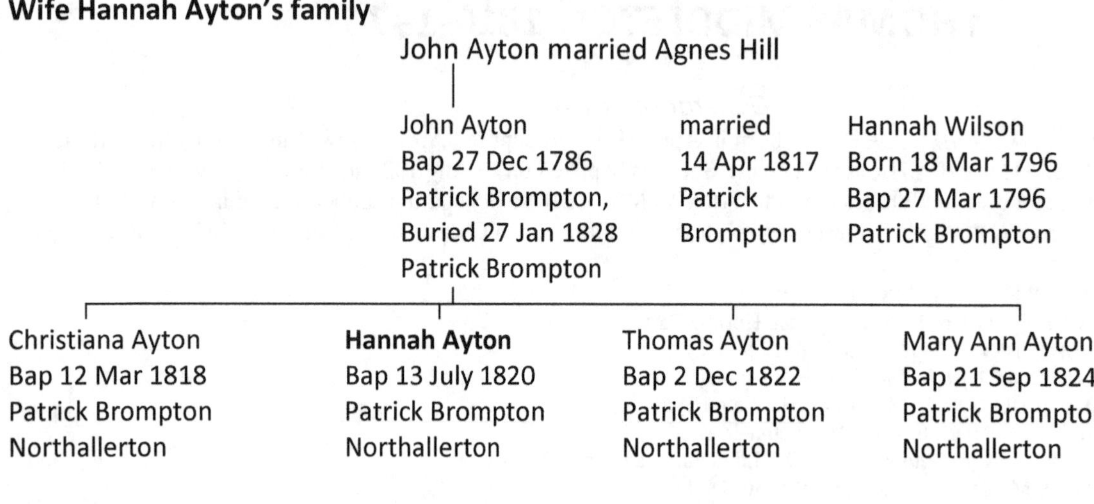

Census day, in 1841, was 6th June and, on that day, Christian or Christiana was living with her younger, married sister Hannah Middleton and her young family. Christian was working as an agricultural labourer and they were all living at Great Fencote/Kirkby Fleetham. Then, shortly after this, on 19th September 1841 Christian marries Robert Ferguson (1802-73) at nearby Bolton-upon-Swale.

Spelling for this family on the 1851 census is Furguson and they are living at Whitwell (still in Richmond, but north east of Brompton) where Robert is described as a Head Farm Servant. Robert was some 16 years older than Christian and had been married before, as the family has a young grandchild, George, living with them at the time.

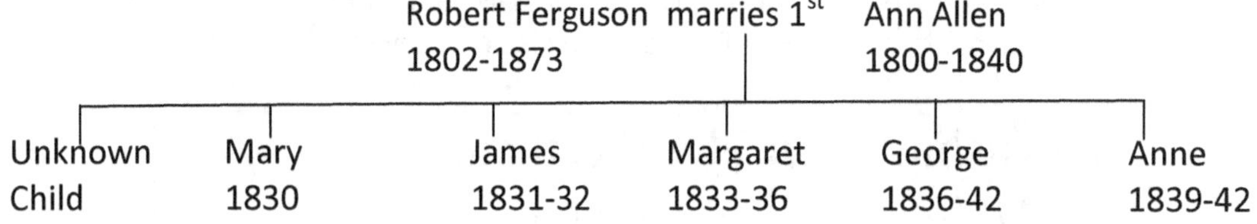

This couple was extremely unlucky to have nearly all their children die as infants. But, from his second marriage to Christiana Ayton, there are many descendants today:

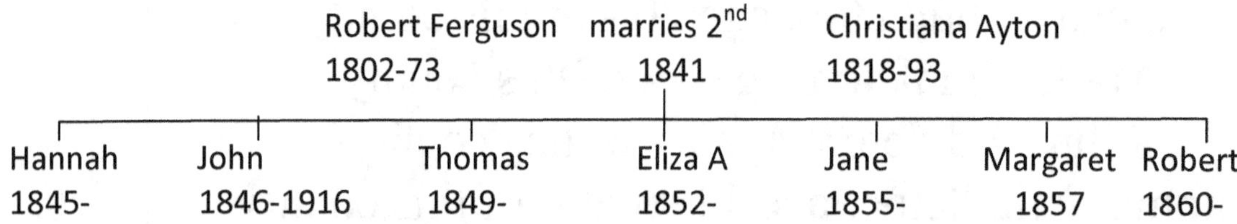

From son John Ferguson 1846-1916, we have the following:-

Robert   Mary E   Jane F   Margaret A   Annie   Isabella   Sarah   Henry   Eva
1873-1949   1874-1953   1880-   1882-1955   1886-   1888-   1890-   1892-   1894-

The next census of 1861 sees the family relocated to White Hills in Scorton (a stone's throw away) where Christiana is referred to as a Hind's wife. Hind is a term used in the north of England and Scotland and usually refers to someone who was a skilled farm labourer, or farm steward and they were quite often given rights to farm cottages.

The couple had seven children and were living at Middleton Tyas by the 1871 census - just a few doors away from Christiana's nephew John Chapman Middleton (who will head up our generation number 6). But, by 1873, Robert (Senior) was dead. Christiana lived on until 1893.

The father of Hannah and Christiana, John Ayton, dies age 42, when Hannah is only 8 years old and is buried at St Thomas's[27] Church in Brompton by Northallerton[28]. There is an entry in the National Wills Index for him, dated 1828, so it may be that he left a will or it may represent a simple probate entry and contain no further information:

Transcript: …. Dated 1828, vol 178, fourth line. August 1828 Ayton John of Brompton P. North Allerton. Prob. 100. The number 100 may be a reference to the value of his estate he left.

The birth of Hannah's father also took place in Patrick Brompton:

John Ayton

27th December 1786

Father's name: John

Father's occupation - blank

Mother's name: Agnes

Abode: Patrick Brompton, Yorkshire

CLEVELAND BAPTISMS. Cleveland Family History Society

He spent his entire 42 years living in this village where his occupation is recorded[29] as being a Weaver.

Siblings

Living just a few houses away from Thomas Middleton, also living at Great Fencote/Kirkby Fleetham, is his younger brother William 1816-1853 living with his wife and two sons: Matthew (who was deaf) and Mark. This family move away from Fencote about 1843 to nearby Melsonby (Mary's home town). Mark b. 1844 was a Blacksmith's apprentice.

Brother John (1808-1902) marries Frances Metcalfe (1819-1903) in 1837. Witnesses at the wedding were siblings William and Hannah. Hannah was literate, though her handwriting is not too fluent but it is an exact match to that on her own wedding record.

---

[27] St Patrick's is the parish church of Patrick Brompton - so record may be incorrectly recorded by Cleveland Family History Society, or, St Mary's Church is nearby in the Hornby district.
[28] Sources: IGI Batch numbers M03998-1, C03998-1, National Burial Index via Cleveland Family History Society and National Wills Index via origins.net
[29] On daughter Christian's baptism record.

It is said that the average American today moves homes 14 times throughout their lives, the average Canadian 10 times and the average Brit just 5 times. Well, when it comes to John Middleton he had difficulty staying anywhere for long as can be seen from the 12 moves he had, with 6 different locations for the births of his children over a 17 year period:-

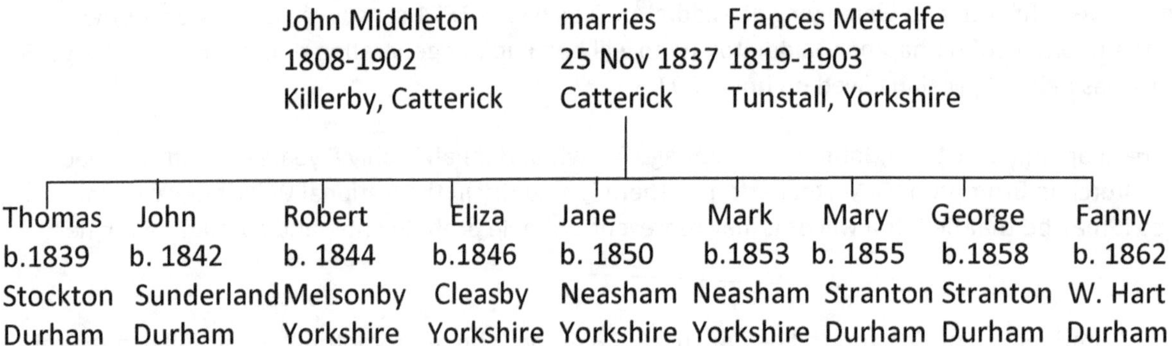

Then, the moving continues through the next 40 years, as the census returns show:-

1841   Brougham Street, Bishopwearmouth, Sunderland - occupation groom
1851   Neasham Grange, Hurworth - agricultural labourer
1861   10 Brunswick Street, Stranton, West Hartlepool - greengrocer
1871   32 Archer Street, Stranton, West Hartlepool
1881   30 Stockton Street, Stranton, West Hartlepool
1891   19 Brown Street, West Hartlepool
1901   19 Brown Street, West Hartlepool - retired market gardener

About the time this family was in Neasham, it was described (in 1848) as follows: "The village consists of one street, extending along the northern bank of the Tees, over which, at this point, are a ferry and two fords."[30] John would probably have lived at a tied cottage on the estate where he was employed.

He does, finally, settle in Hartlepool in his later years and dies in West Hartlepool in 1902 at the ripe old age of 92 years, his wife Frances lived to 84 years.

Descendants

John's daughter Jane Metcalfe Middleton b. 1850 marries a John Parker 1847-1877 and they had a daughter Eliza Jane Parker 1875-1931 who married George T Green 1875-1943. They had a daughter Elizabeth Green 1897-1988 who married Robert Ross 1897-1943. Elizabeth had left school at the age of 14 years to work in Tyler's Bookshop. Then later, prior to marriage, she worked at The British Metal Expansion Company in the Works and Canteen. In later years Elizabeth spent 16 years preparing school dinners. Robert Ross served in WWI on HMS Victory II Crystal Palace and was assigned to torpedo boats. He died in 1943 following an accident at ICI. They had four children.

---

[30] From: 'Neasham - Neswick', A Topographical Dictionary of England (1848), pp. 368-372. URL: http://www.british-history.ac.uk/report.aspx?compid=51168 Date accessed: 19 April 2013

Son John, born in 1842 Sunderland marries Jane Tate in 1862 and they have a son John Robert. Unfortunately Jane dies soon after and by the 1871 census, John Middleton is widowed. The 1881 census though sees him remarried to a Swedish wife, Josephina Tornquist and living at 32 Alma, Stranton, Hartlepool; they go on to have at least two sons Thomas b. 1883 and David b. 1885. Youngest daughter Fanny is, on the 1881 census, working as a servant at the Spotted Cow, Park Street, Stranton. Then, in 1887 she marries a William Coulson (bricklayer). Within one year they have a son Richard Coulson but, at the precise moment when the son is born, Fanny herself dies - so presumably she died at childbirth, or very soon afterwards. Later, we find the infant Richard Coulson living back with his Middleton relations in 1891 and William himself is working away from home. He is working as a Customs Officer at Middlesbrough (Cargo Fleet Toll Bar) and is stated to be widowed, aged just 28 years. So Fanny had a very short, 26 year, life.

Children of Thomas and Hannah

Back to the head of this generation number 4. The birth records of their numerous children show their eldest son Mark being born at Hornby and their second and third sons being born in Kirkby Fleetham. It is difficult to say whether the family was moving around this area - as Hornby and Kirkby Fleetham are only two or three miles apart or, perhaps more likely, they simply chose to baptise their children in different locations. Certainly, though, sometime after the 1841 census, but before the baptism of their son William in 1844, they had moved some fifteen miles north to Middleton Tyas where Thomas and Hannah would have the remainder of their children and spend the rest of their lives there.

Some of the surviving children of Thomas Middleton and Hannah

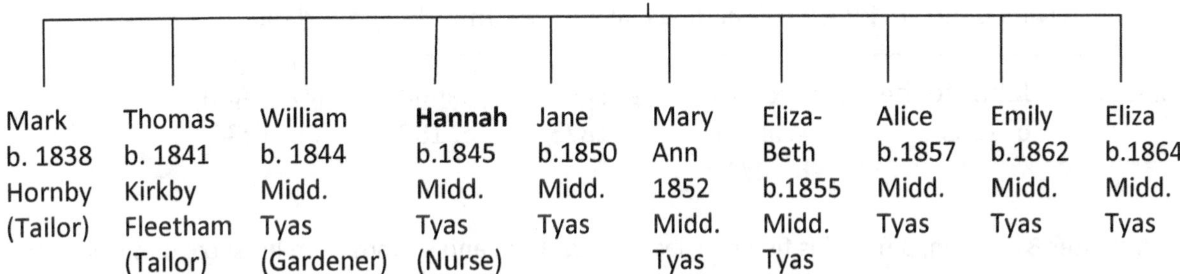

Mark	Thomas	William	**Hannah**	Jane	Mary	Eliza-	Alice	Emily	Eliza
b. 1838	b. 1841	b. 1844	b.1845	b.1850	Ann	Beth	b.1857	b.1862	b.1864
Hornby	Kirkby	Midd.	Midd.	Midd.	1852	b.1855	Midd.	Midd.	Midd.
(Tailor)	Fleetham	Tyas	Tyas	Tyas	Midd.	Midd.	Tyas	Tyas	Tyas
	(Tailor)	(Gardener)	(Nurse)		Tyas	Tyas			

A second son John is born 1839 in Kirkby Fleetham. The two brothers above, Mark b. 1838 and Thomas b. 1841 both marry in 1864 to two women who are also related. Mark marries Elizabeth Fishburn and brother Thomas marries Jane Fishburn (who were sisters/cousins). Both men were working as tailors. On the 1841 census Thomas and Jane are living at No. 12 - front of Hodgsons Buildings, Monkwearmouth Shore in Sunderland with two infants Margaret J born 1865 and Thomas a baby, born 1870. Nearby his brother Mark and Elizabeth are living at 2 Williamson Terrace, Monkwearmouth Shore with three children, Elizabeth J b. 1860, Sarah E, born 1868 and Jno S born 1869. This area would be immediately next to the present-day Sunderland Football Club stadium.

Mark and Thomas: As at 2nd April 1871

Thomas Middleton & Jane Fishburn   **Mark Middleton and Elizabeth Fishburn**
(Living at no. 12, front of Hodgsons Buildings,   (Living at 2 Williamson Terrace,
Monkwearmouth Shore, Sunderland)   Monkwearmouth Shore, Sunderland)

Margaret Jane	Thomas W		Eliz J	Sarah E	Jno S
b. 1865	b. 1870		1860	1868	1869
Monkwearmouth	Oakham				
	Sunderland				

Then, Mark's wife Elizabeth dies later in 1871, at the same time Thomas Middleton himself dies in 1871 aged just 30 years (but after the census was taken on 2nd-3rd April of that year).

Three years later, in 1874, the two widowed Middleton in-laws themselves marry. Jane, the widow of Thomas Middleton marries her widowed brother-in-law, Mark Middleton (the marriage record shows as a Mark Middleton marrying a Jane Middleton). They reside, on the next census, now in the same place that the deceased Thomas (and Jane) had lived, Hodgsons Buildings …

As at Sunday 3rd April 1881:-
Mark Middleton and Jane (Middleton/Fishburn)
(Living at no. 7 Hodgsons Buildings, Monkwearmouth, Sunderland)

Margaret Jane	John Stephen	Thomas	Wilson	Hannah	Mary Ann
b. 1865	b. 1869	William	b. 1875	b. 1877	b. 1880
		b.1871			

Altogether Mark raises 8 children, 3 from his first marriage to Elizabeth and 3 more from his second marriage to Jane as well as Margaret J b. 1865 and Thomas William b. 1870 (who were his brother's children). So, in the case of Margaret J and Thomas William, Mark was both uncle to them and step-father (as they were both his brother's children and his second wife's!)

One puzzling detail - the 1871 census does show Mark's eldest daughter, Elizabeth aged 11 years so she would have been born 1860, which seems strange because he didn't marry until 1864. This is a problem because on the 1861 census Mark was still living with his parents and was unmarried, so either Elizabeth is some other relation or she was born prior to her parents' marriage.

John Stephen Middleton b. 1869 who was living with his Aunt Alice on the 1891 census where he was employed as a Colliery Fireman, marries in 1899 Newcastle to Margaret Mary A Oman. The 1911 census shows him living alone at 4 Clasper Street in Newcastle whilst, at the same time, a few yards away at 29 Water Street, his wife and two sons are recorded as being with her family - of 4 siblings and her widowed mother. It may, of course, be that she was visiting her family on this day rather than having left her husband. John is working as a Shipwright Labourer in the Shipyard - living in 2 rooms - both husband and wife claim their status to be married. He dies in 1917 in Newcastle.

William / Alice:

Other children of Thomas and Hannah: Brother and sister William and Alice Middleton reside together through two census returns. William had married Euphemia Scott (born 1846 in Felton, Northumberland), the couple marry in 1869 at Alnwick. The first census after their marriage shows them living at Low Buston (still in the same area) and William's younger sister Alice is also there ….

As at 2nd April 1871

Residing at Low Buston Cottages, Alnwick

Alice Middleton	William Middleton & (Euphemia Scott)
b. 1857	b. 1844 (Uphance)
Scholar	Gardener/Domestic Servant
	William Middleton
	b. 1871 Shortridge*, Northumberland

* Shortridge is very close to Low Buston.

From the birth records of their children, see 1881 census below, it is possible to track this family's movements and between 1874 and 1877 they move some distance south to relocate to West Boldon in Durham (not too far from South Shields).

As at Sunday 3rd April 1881

Residing at Grange Lodge, Boldon, Durham

Alice Middleton	William Middleton & Euphemia Scott	
b. 1857	b. 1844	b. 1846
Middleton Tyas	Middleton Tyas	Felton, Northumberland
Domestic Service	Market Gardener	

William	James	John	Euphemia
b. 1871	b. 1872	b. 1874	b. 1877
Shortridge	Shortridge	Shortridge	Boldon West
Northumberland	Northumberland	Northumberland	Durham

In addition, there is a John Scott residing with the family. He is Euphemia's nephew - son of her brother Edward born 1835.

As at 5th April 1891

Residing at 39 Wawn Street, Westoe, South Shields

William Middleton and Euphemia

William	John Thomas	Euphemia	Mark E.
b. 1871	b. 1874	b. 1877	b. 1887
Shortridge	Shortridge	Boldon, Durham	Boldon, Durham
Steam Engine Maker	Steam Engine Maker		

By the next census of 1901 the family has moved, yet again, and is now to be found at Ingham Infirmary Lodge in South Shields. William and Euphemia have no more children but son John Thomas Middleton is now employed as a Ship's Engineer. A further two children are still living with their parents, Euphemia (housemaid) and Mark.

The 1911 census shows the family in another house move, living at 23 Readhead Avenue, in South Shields. The only child now still living with William and Euphemia is John Thomas who is now married to Henrietta (b. 1877 in Durham) and the young couple married in 1910. John Thomas' occupation is Seagoing Marine Engineer. On this census return, William and Euphemia claim to have had 9 children (though we can only account for five on the census returns - so some must have died as infants) and that, as at 1911, 4 were alive and 5 had died. The family was living in a house with 4 rooms only.

William died in 1913. Son John Thomas Middleton had at least three girls: Euphemia b. 1914, Elsie b. 1916 and Muriel b. 1919.

Sister Alice Middleton, had left her brother's home and married Edward Scott (b. 1860 Long Horsley, Northumberland) in 1884 in South Shields. Edward was a Railway Signalman. Alice and Edward, by the 1891 census have a young family: Ursula H b. 1886, Alice M. b. 1888 and James E.M. b. 1890, but in addition they have living with them a nephew John Stephen Middleton b. 1869 - he was a Colliery Fireman. (John was the son of Mark Middleton and Elizabeth Fishburn - so his father and Alice were siblings). They have further children (including Florence b. 1895), making a total of 6 in all and they were living at 4 Ebor Street, Simonside, Tyne Dock, Harton in Durham in 1901 and were at the same address in 1911.

Jane Middleton b. 1850

Another daughter of Thomas and Hannah: Jane, b. 1850 was, on the 1871 census, in domestic service at Middleton Lodge to the Backhouse family who were the dominant landowners in Middleton Tyas at this time. She was in service to Edmund Backhouse, M.P., J.P., Banker, Farmer and Landowner.

Middleton Lodge .....

Several Middletons seem to have been in the employ of the Backhouse family at various times. Another Backhouse property, The Rookery (below) in the vicinity, employed John Chapman Middleton (Jane's cousin) (generation 6) and his future wife Maria Bainbridge was also employed there.

It is not known what becomes of the other five daughters born to Thomas and Hannah as there are numerous marriage records that could apply to them.

To finish the review of this generation, we now take a look at the cause of death for the father of the above children, Thomas Middleton 1810-76.   Throughout the census returns for 1851, 1861, 1871, 1881 and 1891 the family remain at Middleton Tyas.   1891 census: address 91 Rose Bank, Middleton Tyas

Thomas Middleton - Cholera Death

Summary of the death certificate for Thomas Middleton:

REGISTRATION DISTRICT: RICHMOND UNION YORKSHIRE
1876 Death in the Sub-District of Richmond in the County of York
Column 1. When and where died: Twenty-second of August 1876 Middleton Tyas.
Name and surname: Thomas Middleton. Sex Male. Age 65 years. Occupation Labourer.
Cause of death English Cholera, certified by W. H. Walker, M.D.
Signature, description and residence of informant: Hannah Middleton, widow of deceased, present at death.
Middleton Tyas.
When registered 1st September 1876. Registrar, M. Sedgwick.

The doctor confirming cause of death identified it as English Cholera - as opposed to the Asiatic cholera which had been introduced to England, mainly from Russia .....

> A barque arrived in the Tyne on Sunday from Russian Finland having on board a seaman suffering from Asiatic cholera. The patient was at once removed to the floating cholera hospital in the river, and the vessel placed in quarantine.

A barque is a sail boat. The above snippet appeared in The Hull Packet on Friday 1st December 1871. Practice was, at the time, to isolate cholera victims, usually preventing the bodies entering churches at death, but going straight to a special 'cholera' area for burial.

At present, we do not know where Thomas was buried. His place of death is stated to be Middleton Tyas and that his wife was present at death, but it is curious that from death it took nine days for the death to be registered. Today the timescale is about 5 days - which a coroner may extend to 14.

By the 1891 census, long after Thomas himself has died, his widow Hannah is still residing in Middleton Tyas and, on that census return, she states her establishment to be four rooms only[31]. So, although the numbers residing at the house went up and down during the decades, it is still a very small house for so large a family. It was not just their own children who lived there, as the 1871 and 1891 census show two grandchildren also living with them - their daughter Hannah's two illegitimate children.

---

[31] There was not much consistency with census enumerators - some would omit to count utility rooms, others would count cupboards as rooms, but generally they were only required to record room numbers in a house when the number was less than five - as overcrowding was becoming a matter of concern.

Hannah (Senior)[32] outlived her daughter Hannah Barker by some fourteen years and also outlives her grand-daughter Louisa Alice who died in 1891. Soon after, her grandson who had been living with her, John Chapman, marries Maria Bainbridge in 1894 and the new-weds move a short distance away to live at Cotherstone. So, it seems likely that for the last 5 or 6 years of her life that Hannah (Senior) was living alone. She dies in 1900[33], Richmond, aged 80 years.

---

[32] Hannah (Senior) daughter of John and Hannah Ayton. John Ayton was a Weaver.
[33] January quarter, 1900, Richmond, volume 9d, page 574.

HANNAH MIDDLETON 1845-1886

Generation No. 5

HANNAH[5] MIDDLETON (*THOMAS[4], MARK[3], JOHN[2], JOHN[1]*) was born May 1845 in Middleton Tyas, North Yorkshire, and died 1886. She married CHRISTOPHER BARKER 1876. He was born 1856 in Hunton, Yorkshire, and died 1930 in Bishop Auckland, Durham.

HANNAH, in 1861, was in service at Uckerby Hall; 1871 in service at Middleton West Hall (nurse). Also had 2 illeg.children before marriage Occupation: Domestic servant

CHRISTOPHER BARKER: Address on 1881 census: 63 Wood Yard, Richmond, Yorkshire

Children of HANNAH MIDDLETON are:

    i.   JOHN CHAPMAN MIDDLETON, b. November 1, 1867, Middleton Tyas

    ii.   LOUISA ALICE MIDDLETON, b. July 24, 1870, Middleton Tyas.

Children of Hannah MIDDLETON and Christopher BARKER are:

    iii.   JANE E. BARKER, b. 1876, Middleton Tyas

    iv.   HANNAH BARKER, b. 1880, Middleton Tyas

    v.   SARAH BARKER, b. 1882, Richmond

    vi.   CHRISTOPHER BARKER, b. 1882, Richmond

    vii.   EMILY MIDDLETON, b. 1885, Great Chilton, near Ferryhill

Birth Record

Hannah is born in 1845 and she heads up our generation number 5. This is a summary of her birth certificate:

> Registration District RICHMOND 1845
> Birth on 15th of April 1845 Middleton Tyas. Name Hannah, girl. Name of father Thomas
> MIDDLETON. Mother's name and maiden surname: Hannah MIDDLETON formerly AYTON,
> rank of father: labourer. Signature, description and residence of informant: T Middleton,
> father, Middleton Tyas. When registered 15th May 1845. E T Atkinson Registrar.

Hannah (daughter of Thomas and Hannah) Middleton was sent out to work in domestic service at a young age, which is not surprising given how large a family she came from and the financial strain on her father, a farm worker. The 1851 census shows her as a child living at home with her family but, by the 1861 census -as a 16 year old house servant, she was in domestic service at Uckerby Hall with the Robinson family who had a butchery business and 213 acres of land to farm. There were three other servants living with the Robinson family as well at the time.

Domestic Service

Ten years later she is still in domestic service, but she is now at West Hall Middleton Tyas where she is engaged as a nurse. The principal landowners of Middleton Tyas, at this time, lived at West Hall and the family was headed up by Leonard Lawrie, Lord Hartley 1816-1883[34] Not only had Hannah changed employment in the ten years since the last census, but she had also given birth to two children, out of wedlock; John Chapman Middleton in 1868 and Louisa in 1870. It's impossible to know the exact sequence of events that took place, but it is likely that Hannah would have been obliged to leave her place of domestic service recorded on the 1861 census at Uckerby Hall due to her pregnancy and, in all likelihood, the only reason she was able to secure a new position at West Hall was because her two infants were being cared for by her mother. The 1871 census shows young John and baby Louisa living with their grandparents John and Hannah - in their overcrowded little house in Middleton Tyas. Just a few doors away from the Middleton household are Robert and Christiana Ferguson

---

[34] Hartley family of Middleton Tyas papers are at North Yorkshire County Record Office

(Hannah's Aunt and Uncle). So these family members took charge of her young children and this enabled Hannah herself to resume work.

Illegitimate Children

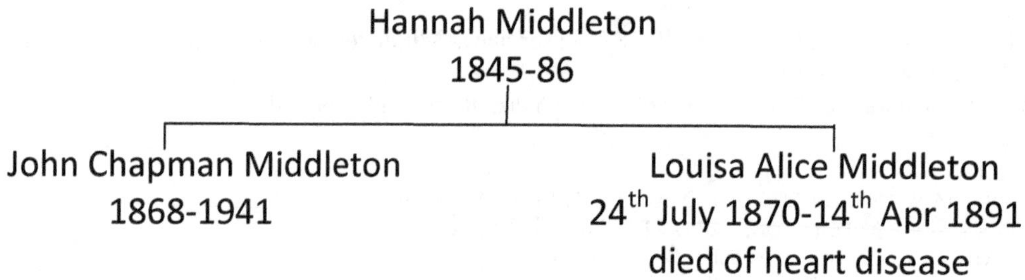

On 24th June 1876 Hannah marries Christopher Barker (baptised 24 August 1856 in Patrick Brompton, near Bedale - parents John/Jane)[35]. His background: on the 1861 census he is living with his family at 19 Church Street, Farmaby, Darlington with father John born 1812, Brompton (labourer at Gas Works), mother Jane, born Muker in 1810 and a sister Margaret, born 1838 in Darlington. By the next census in 1871 he was working in service, being unmarried at that time, at Battery House Farm, Little Crakehall, Bedale (not far from Catterick) working in service to the Atkinson family. He was illiterate and signs the wedding certificate with his "X" mark - occupation farm labourer.

For their marriage, Chris and Hannah are to be found some 40 miles away at 96 Wayman Street, Monkwearmouth in Sunderland. It is likely that they chose this place to marry because Hannah's eldest brother, Mark, and his family were living there. Since banns were read in the Parish Church of All Saints, they must have been resident there at least for a few weeks, but, by the birth of their daughter Jane either in 1877 - anyway very soon after marriage - they are in Middleton Tyas.

Hannah's younger sister, Alice (born 1857) would have been 19 years old at the time of Hannah's wedding, and Alice is present at the wedding, signing the certificate as a witness along with another unknown individual Thomas Stoddard. Hannah signs for herself but Christopher signs with his "X" mark. Christopher states his father as being John Barker, a farm labourer and Hannah states her father to be Thomas Middleton, occupation gardener.

On the 1881 census, Hannah is residing at 63 Wood Yard in Richmond with her husband and four children, that is the two illegitimate children from before her marriage and Jane and Hannah, two infants from her new marriage. With four young children to care for it is likely that she has left domestic service. Her family continues to grow throughout the 1880s.

---

[35] Though he later states his birth place as being Bishop Auckland in census returns. Confirmation of parents' names from his Marriage Certificate.

Descendants of Hannah Middleton (and Christopher Barker)

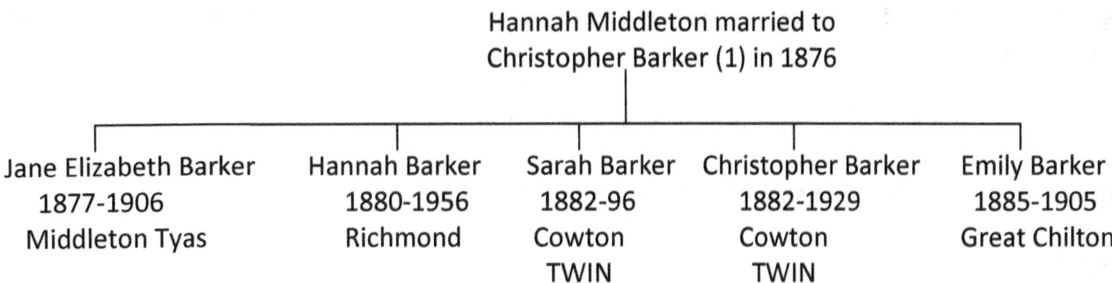

Middleton-Barker Children

Jane Elizabeth Barker (1875-1906) marries Robert Boyd on 4 November 1905 at the Baptist Chapel on Waldron Street in Bishop Auckland. Sister Sarah Barker was a witness at her wedding. On the 1901 census Jane is working in domestic service as a Cook at Quarry Hill in Brancepeth. By the time of her marriage, her address is listed as 40 South Church Road, Bishop Auckland. Witness at her wedding is brother Christopher Barker and a David Boyd, presumably brother to the groom. It is not known what becomes of Robert and Jane after marriage as they are not listed on the 1911 census. However Boyd is a name prominent in Scotland and Ireland, so they may have relocated after marriage; there is a death recorded of a Jane Elizabeth Boyd in 1906 Limerick who would be the right age, being born in 1877. Robert's profession was Millwright (journeyman) and his father was Andrew Boyd, also a Millwright.

Hannah Barker (b. 1879) marries John Binks on 6 June 1903 in Bishop Auckland - she states her address at marriage to be Henknowle (nr Bishop Auckland). This is probably Henknowle Farm (Hindes House) - where her whole family was living on the 1901 census[36]. And the references to "Hindes House" tells us that it would have been a tied cottage they lived in, with father Christopher being employed as "Hind" on the farm, i.e. skilled labourer. Both farm house and cottage are long gone today and the area has been developed over.

It is easy to see how Hannah may have met her future husband as the 1901 census shows John Binks working as a servant to the Gregory family - who were the farmers at Henknowle Farm. Although Hannah herself is not on this census, clearly her family were neighbours to John Binks and the Gregories (farmers). Historical maps show the name Henknowle remaining until about the 1960s when urban spread transformed the area to the point where it is difficult today to believe a farm was ever there.

Husband John states his occupation to be Quarryman and residence South Shields . He is son of Richard Binks (Hind). Hannah's half-sister Minnie May Barker was a witness at the wedding ceremony, the other witness was her brother Christopher Barker(2). The 1911 census shows them in Sedgefield and that John and Hannah had produced 3 children by that time, but only 2 of them survived: Isabella born 1907 in Ferryhill, Durham and John

---

[36] Henknowle Farm (Hindes House) Auckland St Andrew. Piece 4646, folio 46, page 32.

Robert Binks born in 1910 also at Ferryhill. Hannah's address on the 1911 census was 11 Saddler Street, Ferryhill, County Durham with the family living in 2 rooms only! Husband John Binks is working as a colliery worker (above ground). Although Saddler Street still exists, it has been partially redeveloped and the original house at no. 11 is no longer there.

Isabella Binks b. 1906 Ferryhill marries John W Woods around August 1924 in Sedgefield. They have three children: Ivy, Margaret and Allan E. It is likely that both Ivy and Margaret marry, but no descendants have been traced. Allan E Binks dies at birth.

John Robert Binks b. 1920 Ferryhill marries around May 1936 to Elizabeth B Davison .

Sarah Barker (b. 1882) - alive at 1905 (witness at sister Jane Elizabeth's wedding).

Christopher Barker (2)

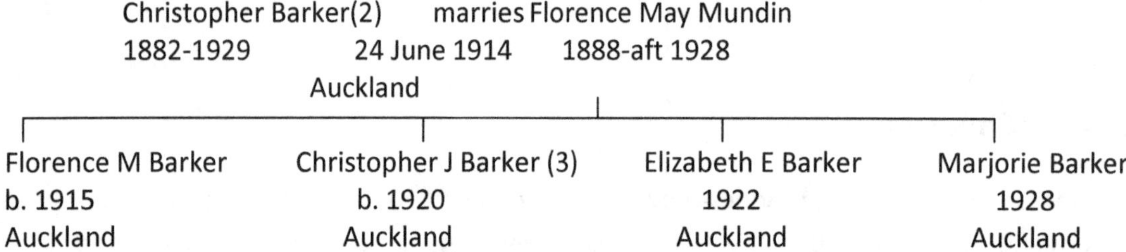

Christopher Barker (Junior) marries Florence May Mundin at the Wesleyan Methodist Church, South Road, Bishop Auckland in Durham on 24th June 1914. He states his profession to be Stonemason and his address is 6 St Andrew's Crescent and his father to be Christopher Barker (Senior), occupation labourer.

Emily Barker (1885-1900)

Death of Hannah Barker (nee Middleton)

Hannah dies in 1886, at 41 years of age after giving birth to seven children[37].

Burial of Hannah Barker on 22 November 1886

at Croft (near Richmond) at St Peter's

Death Certificate for Hannah says ….

REGISTRATION DISTRICT DARLINGTON
1886 Death in the Sub-district of Darlington in the Counties of Durham and York
No. 381 When and where died: 19th November 1886 at Dalton. Name and surname: Hannah Barker. Female.
40 years. Occupation - wife of Christopher Barker, farm labourer. Cause of death: Phthisis 1 year. Certified by W. Chisholm M.D. Signature, description and residence of informant - C. Barker, widower of deceased, present

---

[37] National Burial Index.

at death, Dalton. When registered 20th November 1886. Registrar, William Savill.

Cause of death for Hannah: Phthisis - is pulmonary tuberculosis - TB.

St Peter's Church, Croft-on-Tees, where Hannah is buried, had as its rector 1843-68 Lewis Carroll's father and it is believed the church has connections with the Milbank family - owners of Snape Castle at the time. Pauline Batty visited St Peter's Church in Croft in March 2013 but the Churchwarden confirmed that, although records show Hannah was buried there, no headstone sadly had been erected at the time of her death.

Within two years of Hannah's demise, Christopher Barker has remarried to Elizabeth Dixon[38] and he has further children: Minnie in 1890 (Ferryhill), followed by twins John and Thomas in 1891 (born Great Chilton), William in 1893 (Richmond) and, after a long 17 year interval, lastly, Harold Alvey Barker 1909-2000, born in Bishop Auckland. After Hannah's death, Christopher Barker keeps his own children, but Hannah's two illegitimate children are found, on the next census return, living back with their grandmother, also called Hannah (born 1822) living at The Rookery where John Chapman Middleton is supporting them all.

On the 1901 census the Barker family is living at Henknowle Farm, Hindes House, Auckland St Andrew.[39] By the 1911 census the family has relocated to 6 St Andrew's Crescent, Bishop Auckland[40]

The census shows Christopher and family (8 persons in total) living in 4 rooms. The family was all manual workers: Christopher Senior (b.1854) was working as a highways labourer for the Rural District Council, son Christopher Junior (b. 1882) was a bricklayer, as was younger brother John (b. 1891). Thomas (b. 1891) was a Cartman and William (b. 1893) was working at a Blacksmith's Forge.

Christopher Barker (Senior) dies in 1930 in Bishop Auckland.

---

[38] 24th November 1888, St Anne's Church, St Andrew's Parish, Bishop Auckland. M01657-2 IGI.
[39] Piece 4646, folio 46, page 32.
[40] RG14, pc 29707.

JOHN CHAPMAN MIDDLETON
1867-1941

Generation No. 6

JOHN CHAPMAN[6] MIDDLETON (*HANNAH[5], THOMAS[4], MARK[3], JOHN[2], JOHN[1]*) was born November 1, 1867 in Middleton Tyas, North Yorkshire, and died September 1941 in Darlington. He married MARIE BAINBRIDGE September 1894 in St Mary's Church, South Cowton, Yorkshire. She was born 1871 in North Cowton, and died April 1941 in Darlington. He was the illegitimate son of Hannah. 1901 census: 77 New Town, Cotherstone, Yorkshire Occupation: Gardener

Children of JOHN MIDDLETON and MARIE BAINBRIDGE are:
    i.   AMY[7] MIDDLETON, b. 1896, Cotherstone
    ii.   MABEL MIDDLETON, b. December 1897, Cotherstone
    iii.   EDITH ANN MIDDLETON, b. September 24, 1899, Cotherstone
    iv.   MARY MIDDLETON, b. 1902, Cotherstone
    v.   LOUISA ALICE MIDDLETON, b. December 7, 1905
    vi.   WILFRED MIDDLETON, b. 1910, Darlington
    vii.   DOUGLAS RAYMOND MIDDLETON, b. September 4, 1918, Darlington

Pictured right ……. John Chapman Middleton, eldest son of Hannah and, like sister Louisa, born illegitimately.

Birth Record
John Chapman Middleton was born 1st November 1867 in Middleton Tyas.

Although John was born, and spent his early life in Middleton Tyas, it seems likely that he would have had quite an unsettled upbringing, as his mother's domestic service duties would have entailed the family moving with her.

He was just 9 years of age when his mother marries Christopher Barker and immediately begins a new, large family.

Then, just 10 years (and seven children) later, his mother dies when he is only 19 years of age.

Pictured supplied by Audrey Dyke nee Seton who is John's granddaughter (via Louise b.1906)

At this point, he moves away from the Barker home and takes up employment at The Rookery, in Middleton Tyas. By the next census, in 1891, he seems to be the only person in his household in employment - as he is engaged as a gardener at The Rookery, but living with him is his 70 year old widowed grandmother Hannah and his ailing sister Louisa. Louisa, aged just 24, dies within weeks of the 1891 census and had been suffering heart problems for many, many years. So it seems that John was supporting both of these women from an early age. According to Louisa's death certificate, it was John who was with her at the time of her death.

Left: **Marie Bainbridge** in later years, John's wife. In the 1891 census, we can see how these two met. Amongst others, they were employed at The Rookery in Middleton Tyas - an elegant country mansion built in 1797 and home of Sir Edmund Trelawny Backhouse (1873-1944), "the most extravagant character ever born in the village of Middleton Tyas".[41] They were a family in the banking industry but Sir Edmund was known to have had an affair with Oscar Wilde. Here we find, on the census, Maria Bainbridge, single, aged 19 years, occupation domestic servant to Jonathan (son of Edmund) and Florence Backhouse and John Chapman Middleton is employed as the gardener.

So, after the early death of his mother in 1886, then his sister in 1891, John has lost some of his closest family. Soon after, however, in September 1894 he marries Marie Bainbridge and they had seven children:

John Chapman Middleton and Marie Bainbridge
marry 1894 Cotherstone

Amy	Mabel	Edith	Mary	Louisa Alice	Wilfred	Douglas
b.1896	b.1897	b.1899	b.1902	b.1906	b.1910	b.1918
Cotherstone	Cotherstone	Cotherstone	Cotherstone	Darlington	Darlington	Darlington

On their marriage certificate, John Chapman Middleton states his father's name to be John Middleton, occupation gardener, though of course his own birth certificate makes no identification whatsoever for his father, so it is thought that this was some "creative thinking" by John Chapman and, perhaps, some face-saving on his wedding day in front of his wife's family. Probably easier to invent a father, than say you were illegitimate!

After marriage, the couple move 18 miles away from Middleton Tyas to 77 New Town[42], Cotherstone where most of their children are born. John continues working as a domestic gardener. Then around 1905 they move some 25 miles away to Darlington - perhaps for John to commence his gardening duties with the Scott family at Danby Lodge, their daughter Louisa Alice is born there on 7th December 1905.

---

[41] Northern Echo, 4 April 2011.
[42] 1901 and 1911 Census John Scott at Danby Lodge.

Fairfield Nursing Home

Curiously, the 1911 Census shows John residing as a patient at the Fairfield Nursing Home in Darlington (it is speculation as to why he was there - illness, recuperation from illness etc) but it is thought it was a short-term stay. His wife and children at this time were living at Danby Lodge Cottages on Cleveland Avenue in Darlington.

Now converted to 2-3 houses, the building [43] is situated at 27 Staindrop Road, Darlington at the junction with Carmel Road North and Staindrop Road. It was used as some sort of convalescent home around the time of the First World War.[44]

Danby Lodge Cottages

Right: Danby Lodge Cottages.

This, now modernized and extended house, is where John and his family lived in his employer's cottage, whilst he worked as a gardener initially for Sir John Scott. It was a tied cottage which would have been in the grounds of nearby Danby Lodge itself.

Today there has been much development and building in the area around the cottages, but it would originally have stood within, or on the perimeter, of his employer's estate. On early maps, held at Darlington Library, the property can be seen as "Danby Lodge Cottages Black Path" - the path being a walkway from the big house to the cottages.

---

[43] 1911 Census.

[44] Picture reproduced, with thanks and with permission, from **Colin Bainbridge** www.AboutDarlington.co.uk

Danby Lodge Gardener

John was illiterate, his Will being marked with an "X" by him after it had been read aloud to him for his approval. Throughout his working life he was employed as a gardener and, during the period 1907-13[45], he was employed by Sir John Scott (1855-1922) who probably had Danby Lodge built in 1903.

Right: 16 room[46] Danby Lodge today is a nursing home

The house was possibly named for Sir John Scott's wife Elizabeth, who was born in Danby, Yorkshire.[47] Sir John was the son of Sir Walter Scott (1826-1910) "one of the greatest regional civil engineering contractors of his era".

Walter Scott was only created 1st Baronet of Beauclerk in 1907 (just three years before he died). At which time, the title passed to his eldest son Sir John who became 2nd Baronet of Beauclerk of Bywell St Andrews, Northumberland from 1910 until his own death in 1922. Amongst other projects, Sir John was responsible for the building of the Vittoria Docks at Birkenhead.[48] This, then, was John Chapman Middleton's employer.

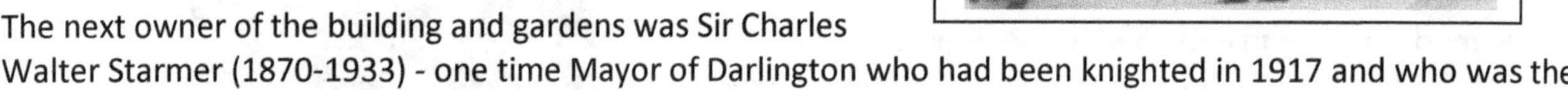

Right: John and wife Marie taken on a day trip to Whitley Bay. Both would die in 1941, Marie died five months before John.

After the demise of Sir John Scott, John must have continued his job as gardener working at the Danby Lodge estate.   It is thought John had an Inheritance from the Will of his employer, who left bequests to certain members of staff.[49]

The next owner of the building and gardens was Sir Charles Walter Starmer (1870-1933) - one time Mayor of Darlington who had been knighted in 1917 and who was the

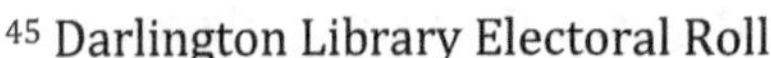

[45] Darlington Library Electoral Roll

[46] See 1911 census

[47] Ibid.

[48] It took four years to complete and, in 1909, just before it was finished, an accident occurred. Sea water rushed over a temporary dam that had been erected to protect workers putting the finishing touches to the project. 14 men drowned.

[49] The Times: Thursday 6th July 1922 (page 13, column d). Sir John Scott Bt, of Danby Lodge, Darlington, Durham, the well known contractor, who carried out many contracts for the construction of reservoirs, docks and other works, head of Walter Scott and Middleton Limited and of the Tyne Brass and Tuber Manufacturing Company, Jarrow, who died on April 29th, in his 68th year, left a fortune of £582,165 the net personalty being £563,064. The Testator gives £1,000 to the Queen's Nursing Association, Darlington. All his wearing apparel to his male servants; £250 each to his butler Ralph Murcaster, and his wife, **his head gardener**, his coachman and his chauffeur. And £10 for each year of service to all his indoor and outdoor servants.

proprietor of numerous newspapers. It is thought that when he died, in 1933[50], John continued in his employment working for Lady Starmer.

Grand-daughters Audrey Dyke b.1933 and Barbara Beckwith b.1926 both recall this. Therefore it is highly likely that John remained working for the same house/estate as a gardener for the remainder of his working life.

In 1922 John and his family leave Danby Lodge Cottages and purchase their own house at 24 Wycombe Street in Darlington.

On 10th September 1941 John Chapman dies of heart failure and chronic bronchitis. Present at his death was daughter Louisa Alice Setton. His occupation: retired domestic gardener.

Picture right - is John Chapman Middleton[51].
In the above picture he is seen posing with "the largest fish ever caught on the River Tees", near Blackwell - at least, that's the tale that has been passed down in the family.

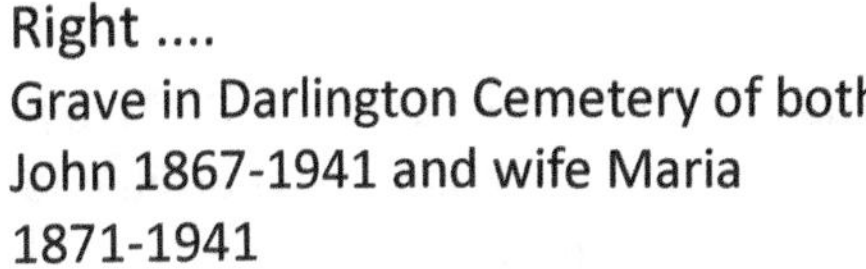

Right ....
Grave in Darlington Cemetery of both John 1867-1941 and wife Maria 1871-1941

Probate

MIDDLETON, John Chapman of 24 Wycombe Street, Darlington Died 10 September 1941. Probate Durham 10 November to Louise Alice Seton (wife of Edward Seton) and Walter Rushbrook[52] carting contractor. Effects £386 5s 11d.

Daughter Louisa, who herself dies in 1958, is included in the above grave and mentioned on the headstone.

---

[50] Probate: Sir Charles Walter Starmer, Knight of Danby Lodge Darlington, died 27 June 1933 at 57 Tufton Street, Westminster, Middx. Probate: Durham 13 October to Dame Mary Cecilia Wakefield Starmer, widow and Frederick Reed, newspaper manager. Effects £63,372 6s 2d.
[51] Both Laura and Elsie Dinsdale had copies of this photograph handed down to them.
[52] Lived on the next street to John and was a coal merchant.

Last Will and Testament of John Chapman Middleton

This is the Last Will of me John Chapman Middleton of 24 Wycombe Street, Darlington in the County of Durham made this twenty-ninth day of August one thousand nine hundred and forty one.

1.1 I hereby revoke all former Wills and testamentary dispositions at any time heretofore made by me.

2.1 I appoint my daughter Louisa Alice Seton and Walter Rushbrooke of 9 Napier Street Darlington aforesaid, Carting Contractor, to be the executors and trustees of this my Will.

3.1 I give devise and bequeath all my real and personal estate whatsoever and wheresoever and of what nature of kind so ever unto my trustees upon trust to sell call in and convert into money the same or such part thereof as shall not consist of money and stand possessed of the proceeds of such sale calling in and conversion together with my ready monies (hereinafter called "my trust funds") Upon trust after paying there out my just debts funeral and testamentary expenses to divide the residue between my daughter Mary Middleton and my son Douglas Raymond Middleton in equal shares if they both shall be living at the date of my death but in case only one of them shall be then living then in trust for that one absolutely.

4.1 Provided always that in case both the said Mary Middleton and Douglas Raymond Middleton shall die in my lifetime then my trustees shall stand possessed of my trust funds upon trust for such of my children who may be living at my decease in equal shares and share alike if more than one and if only one then for that one absolutely.

In witness whereof I have hereunto set my hand the day and year first before written.
John Chapman Middleton ______________________ his mark.

Signed by the said John Chapman Middleton as and for his last Will, the contents of the above written Will having been first read over and explained to him and he being unable to write made his mark hereto in the presence of us both being present at the same time who in his presence at his request and in the presence of each other have hereunto subscribed our names as witnesses.
Marjory Laws, 26 Wycombe Street, Darlington, Co. Durham ___________ Practical Milliner.
Freda Housey (Miss) 18 Wycombe Street, Darlington., Co. Durham ______ Munition Worker
Fos.b.

On the 10th November 1941 PROBATE of this Will was granted at Durham.
Certified Copy.

Children of John Chapman Middleton and Marie

Amy Middleton - Eldest Child 1896-1952
7th Generation

Amy was born 1896 in Cotherstone, Yorkshire. Her first marriage was in 1920 to Ernest Boyes but, unfortunately he dies some months later in 1921. She marries, secondly in 1924 to Jacob Tallentire at Darlington. They had two daughters, Muriel in 1925 and Jean in 1931. Amy dies in 1952 in Darlington.

Picture supplied by Amy's daughter Muriel

Mabel Middleton (2nd daughter) 1897-1951
7TH Generation

Mabel was born in December 1897 in Cotherstone, Yorkshire where her family were living prior to their arrival in Darlington in 1906. Mabel marries George Desmond Hutchinson (1897-1982) who was born in Easington, County Durham.
As a young, single man, George had been living with his family at 31 South Street in Spennymoor when he was called up for service in the First World War during 1916. However, an illness which had taken place when he was just 12 years old, was to limit him to manual labour in England during war-time and led to his early discharge from military service. In 1909 he had suffered a bout of pneumonia and, shortly after that, he began to suffer problems with his eyesight. An Army Medical Officer who examined him said the following:-

"This man tells me he suffered from pneumonia in 1909 and shortly afterwards he complained of his sight which has gradually got worse, especially during the last 18 months since he enlisted. He complains of pain in the left eye but not the right .... it has not been caused, but has been aggravated, by service during the present war."

George served in the Army from 11 October 1916 to 10 April 1918 as a Private. He signed his enlistment papers with his mark "X" being unable to read or write throughout his life. He stated his occupation as "spare cartman", that he was 19 years and 8 months old when he joined up at Newcastle and that he was single. He was given medical clearance, BII, at joining and his regimental number was 219209 when he was assigned to the ASC - Army Service Corps (Loader-Issuers). His father was stated to be George Hutchinson, his height 5ft 4.5" and he was assigned to work as a labourer at the Woolwich Dockyard which at that time was a hive of war-time activities employing some 80,000 people. Personal details: complexion dark, eyes blue, hair dark brown and military character was stated to be good. He was discharged in 1918 with optic atrophy and was discharged as being no longer physically fit for service due to deteriorating eye sight.

Mabel has two daughters Barbara b. 1926 and Dorothy 1932-2012.

Edith Annie Middleton (3rd daughter) will be discussed later.

Other Middleton Children .... Louisa, Douglas, Edith and Mary

7th Generation

Left to right: Louisa 1905-58, Douglas 1918-93, Edith 1899-1972 & Mary 1902-70 MIDDLETON Picture was
taken at the marriage of Audrey SETTON (Louisa's daughter)
to Joseph Kenneth DYKES on 2nd July 1955 Picture supplied by Moira HOLLIS (nee BLADES) Identification of
individuals by Audrey DYKES (nee SETON)

Louisa 1905-58 marries Edward Seton in 1930 and has two daughters.

Douglas Middleton 1918-93 worked on a market stall in Darlington, he married Doreen Stobart in 1951.

Mary 1902-70 remained unmarried and lived at her father's house at 24 Wycombe Street. Mary suffered badly
with arthritis and had worked in a fruit shop in Skinner Gate, Darlington.

Edith Annie Middleton 1899-1972 ......

Third daughter of John Chapman and Marie Middleton, Edith was born in 1899 and the following picture (on the left) was taken when she would have been about 16 years old:

- The picture on the right (with Edith on the right with a friend or work colleague) may date from around 1918 when it looks as if both girls were factory workers – perhaps doing munitions work for WWI. *Picture supplied by Moira Hollis (grand-daughter) (daughter of Elsie Dinsdale)*

In 1919 Edith marries Edwin Dinsdale (Jnr) - see picture right. This picture must have been taken in 1922 and shows Edith (aged 23), Edwin (aged 27) with two youngest daughters Elsie (age 3 yrs) sitting on her father's lap and Laura (age 1) sitting on her mother's knee.

Picture courtesy of Roslyn Semple (grand-daughter)

Edwin Dinsdale's family arrived in Darlington in 1890 and Edwin, like his father, went to work for the largest company in Town, the Darlington Forge Company. In 1912-13 he signed up for military service with the Durham Light Infantry and spends the next few years serving his country. He spent Christmas 1915 in France with his unit and, by 1917, was made Lance Corporal. After receiving medals, he was discharged from military service in 1918 and returned to the Forge Company. Within a year he had married Edith. Edwin and Edith have six children; five girls and one boy (including twins).

Children of EDITH MIDDLETON and EDWIN DINSDALE are:
  i.   ELSIE DINSDALE, b. 1919; d. 1984, Darlington.
  ii. LAURA DINSDALE, b. 1921, Darlington; d. 1997, Derby.
  iii. MARJORIE ELEANOR DINSDALE, b. 1923; d. 1988, Darlington
  iv. MAURICE DINSDALE, b. 1923, Darlington; d. 1993, Darlington.
  v.   JOYCE DINSDALE, b. 1928, Darlington; d. 1972, Darlington.
  vi. MAUREEN DINSDALE, b. 1931; d. 2002, Darlington

Edwin was one of the first to join the Local Defence Volunteers when it was formed in 1940 (Dad's Army) and remained with them until it was disbanded in 1945. Edwin dies of cancer in 1946 in Darlington.

A little while later Edith re-marries to Edwin's brother
Arnold 1888-1953
 (Arnold had a prosthetic right hand)
He kept pigs on a piece of land near the
family home and worked as a plumber.

Picture courtesy of Pauline BATTY

Edith Annie was close to Arnold's family and, even though they were only married for five years before his death, she makes bequests to Arnold's children in her Will.

LAST WILL AND TESTAMENT

This is the Last Will of me EDITH ANNIE DINSDALE of 34 Kirkstall Crescent Darlington in the County of Durham widow made this Twelfth day of August One Thousand Nine Hundred and Fifty Eight.

I APPOINT my brother Douglas Middleton and my sister Mary Middleton (hereinafter called my Trustees) Executors and Trustees of this my Will.

I BEQUEATH to my stepson Walter Dinsdale a legacy of Five Pounds.

I BEQUEATH my shares in Tees Side Farmers to my stepson Eric Dinsdale and my stepdaughter Irene Dinsdale in equal shares absolutely.

I GIVE all my estate both real and person not otherwise disposed of by this my Will unto my Trustees upon trust to sell the same (with power to postpone sale) and out of the moneys to arise from such sale and my ready money to pay my funeral, testamentary expenses legacy and debts and divide the residue between all my children in equal shares PROVIDED that if any child of mine shall die in my lifetime leaving issue living at my decease and who attain twenty one years then such issue shall take and if more than one equally between them the share in my residuary estate his her or their parent would have taken if such parent had survived me.
I REVOKE all Wills at any time heretofore made by me.

IN WITNESS whereof I have hereunto set my hand the day and year first above written.
Signed Edith Annie Dinsdale

SIGNED by the said Edith Annie Dinsdale as her last Will in the presence of us present at the same time who at her request in her presence and in the presence of each other we have hereunto subscribed our names as witnesses.

M James -   Clerks to Messrs Clayhills Lucas & Co., Solicitors, Darlington
D Bower -

It is curious that Edith Annie refers to herself as "Dinsdale" in her Will which was drawn up in 1958 because, in fact, she had married for a third time in 1955 to Harry Dunn. Perhaps she had a premonition of what was to transpire many years later - Harry Dunn was not, in fact, free to marry - already having a living wife who he had not divorced.

Edith leaves specific bequests to her second husband's family - her step-children: to all three of Arnold's children: Eric, Irene and Walter Dinsdale, with the bulk of her estate to be sold off and divided equally between her own children.

Edith dies on 17th May 1972 and probate is granted on 20th June 1972 on an estate worth £841.09 (net £732.92) to the Executor Douglas Raymond Middleton of 22 Oaklands Terrace, Darlington. Probate granted by the High Court, district probate Newcastle upon Tyne.

Edith is buried with her first husband Edwin ....

Right: Two of Edwin & Edith's Grandchildren:
Pauline BATTY and Graham PROUDLER
at the grave of Edwin & Edith Dinsdale

Taken July 2009

Children of Edith Middleton

Edith Middleton and her husband Edwin Dinsdale had one son and five daughters – here is mum with five daughters:

Left to right: Laura, Elsie, (Mum=Edith Ann Middleton), Marjorie, Maureen (head shot only) and Joyce.

Taken at Moira's wedding (grand-daughter) on 26th August 1967.

Picture supplied by Pauline BATTY

And, son Maurice .....

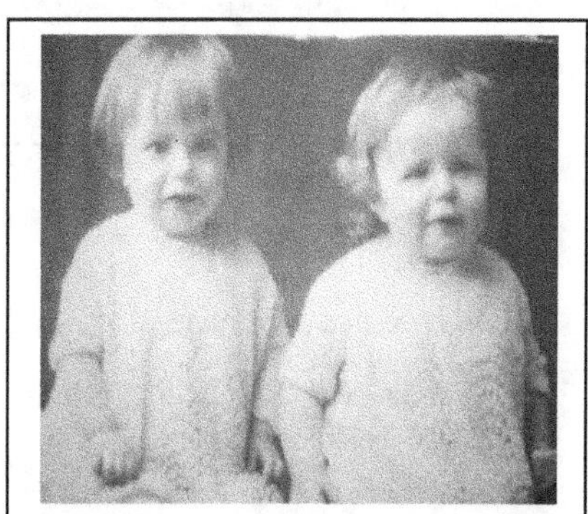

Twins: Maurice Edwin DINSDALE (1923-93) and right: Marjorie Eleanor DINSDALE (1923-88)
Picture supplied by Michael and Dianne PROUDLER, identification by Pauline BATTY

Generation No. 9

MAURICE EDWIN[9] DINSDALE *(EDWIN[8], EDWIN[7], COLLINGWOOD[6], JAMES[5], JOSEPH[4], JOHN[3], JOSEPH[2], THOMAS[1])* was born July 23, 1923 in Darlington, and died February 1993 in Darlington. He married DOREEN HOLMAN July 1948 in Durham East. Twin with Marjorie Eleanor.

Child of MAURICE DINSDALE and DOREEN HOLMAN is:
      i.   MAURICE E[10] DINSDALE, b. March 1948; m. ? WARDMAN, 1987, Darlington.

Elsie Dinsdale (1919-1984)

Generation No. 9

ELSIE[9] DINSDALE *(EDWIN[8], EDWIN[7], COLLINGWOOD[6], JAMES[5], JOSEPH[4], JOHN[3], JOSEPH[2], THOMAS[1])* was born October 6, 1919 in Darlington, and died December 1984 in Darlington. She married WILLIAM HENRY BLADES October 1939 in Darlington. He was born May 6, 1917 in Gateshead and died February 19, 1999 in Darlington.

Children of ELSIE DINSDALE and WILLIAM BLADES are:
112.   i.   MALCOLM[10] BLADES, b. April 28, 1947, Darlington.
113.   ii. MOIRA PATRICIA BLADES, b. August 1, 1950.

Elsie above left, and right with husband Harry BLADES (taken on wedding day) October 1939. It is thought that Elsie worked at a Chemicals Factory in Darlington at some point.
(Picture supplied by Moira Hollis – their daughter)

Laura Dinsdale (1921-1997)

Generation No. 9

LAURA[9] DINSDALE (*EDWIN[8], EDWIN[7], COLLINGWOOD[6], JAMES[5], JOSEPH[4], JOHN[3], JOSEPH[2], THOMAS[1]*) was born February 11, 1921 in Darlington, and died January 23, 1997 in Derby. She married (1) STANLEY QUINTIN November 1942 in Darlington. He was born February 14, 1920 in Edmonton, London, and died October 1997 in Enfield, Middlesex. She married (2) JOHN WILLIAM PROUDLER March 1948 in Derby. He was born December 15, 1923 in Derby, and died August 2011 in Derby. JOHN WILLIAM PROUDLER: Died of asbestosis (life-long worker at Derby Loco Works, British Rail)

Children of LAURA DINSDALE and JOHN PROUDLER are:
  i.   MICHAEL PROUDLER, b. December 23, 1945, Derby
  ii. GRAHAM JOHN PROUDLER, b. July 11, 1949, Derby

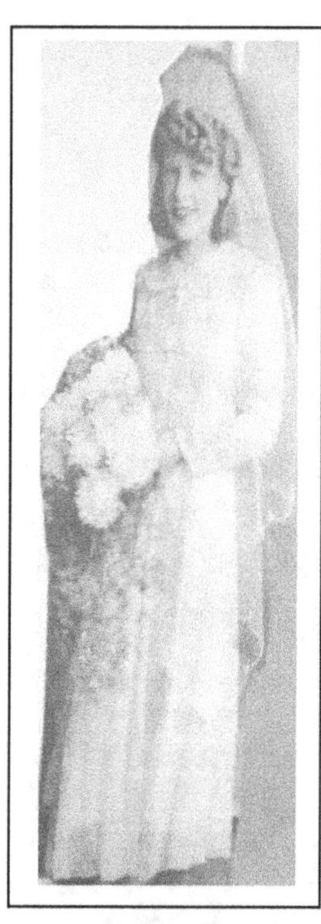

Laura, above in WWII military uniform and right (in her wedding dress from her first marriage to Stanley Quentin in Darlington in 1942 at St John's Church). It was said by a guest at this wedding (who shall remain nameless), that Laura slapped the groom across the face at the reception![53]

Left: Laura married second husband John William PROUDLER (1923-2011) in 1948 Derby where they lived.
John (Jack) died in 2011 of asbestosis caused by his life-time working at British Rail. Jack and Laura divorced in the 1980s but neither remarried. Laura moved to Darlington for some years before finally returning to Derby where she died in 1997.
Son Michael was born 1945 and Graham 1949.

---

[53] Same person remembers Laura coming home to Darlington in her war-time uniform, on leave.

Laura used to tell a story about being chased down Vale Street in Derby, during the Second World War, by a Nazi plane which was shooting at her. She hid in what she called Scattergood's entry (a house across the road from her home at the time) and son Graham recalls being shown the bullet holes in the building many years later. The following newspaper article confirms Laura's story ....

"NEWS IN BRIEF:
CIVILIANS SHOT BY ENEMY AIRCRAFT Monday 27th July 1942

Twenty-two civilians were killed and many more injured in a terrifying attack by a lone enemy aircraft today. At 7.50 am the Dornier 217 skimmed the roof tops of Rolls-Royce with bomb doors open and machine guns blazing. Two bombs caused considerable damage to stores, workshops and houses opposite the works.

The aircraft then turned its attention to Osmaston Road and surrounding streets where it gunned down workers. It then flew towards Friar Gate area where the Babbington Lane barrage balloon was shot down and a bus in Slack Lane machine-gunned".

Laura, dressed in her army uniform, was spotted by the plane and shot at. Her location would have been right on the plane's path, after leaving Rolls Royce, it would have flown over Vale Street on its way to Friar Gate. Rolls Royce was producing the Merlin engine at the time, which powered the Hurricane and Spitfire aircraft, but this was the only German aircraft to ever successfully hit the Rolls Royce factory throughout World War II. Of the four bombs it dropped, one hit the factory and the other three hit residential houses and shops, causing the biggest loss of life in Derby during the War.

Son Graham b.1949 & wife Karen

***Remembrance Tree planted near Ednaston,
Derbyshire for Laura ....***

Marjorie Eleanor Dinsdale (1923-1988)

Generation No.9

MARJORIE ELEANOR DINSDALE *(EDWIN[8], EDWIN[7], COLLINGWOOD[6], JAMES[5], JOSEPH[4], JOHN[3], JOSEPH[2], THOMAS[1])* was born July 23, 1923 in Darlington and died June 1988 in Darlington. She married (1) JOHN MARSHALL ANDREW June 2, 1941 in Darlington. He was born 1918, and died January 1944 in Darlington. She married (2) FRANK PECKITT June 2, 1945 in St Johns Church, Darlington. He was born July 15, 1923 in Howgrave, Yorkshire, and died June 1979 in Darlington.

Address at marriage 24 Wycombe Street, Darlington. Sister Laura was a witness at her first marriage to John M Andrew. Twin (with Maurice). Buried West Cemetery, Darlington

More About JOHN MARSHALL ANDREW: Notes Died of throat cancer. Occupation: Steelworker.

Child of MARJORIE DINSDALE and JOHN ANDREW is:
      i.   JOHN EDWIN ANDREW, b. December 13, 1941.

Child of MARJORIE DINSDALE and FRANK PECKITT is:
      ii.   PAULINE[10] PECKITT, b. January 5, 1946, Greenbank Hospital, Darlington.

Wedding of Marjorie Eleanor
DINSDALE to Frank Peckitt
2 June 1945 at Darlington

Marjorie marries Edwin Andrew in 1941 and they have a son John Edwin Andrew born 13 December 1941. Edwin, sadly, dies of throat cancer in 1944. Marjorie marries, secondly, to Frank Peckitt in 1945. They have a daughter Pauline (b. 1946)

Family of Marjorie Eleanor and Frank Peckitt

10th generation

Above: Marjorie's daughter Pauline at her marriage to John BATTY in 7 March 1964.

Joyce Mary Dinsdale (1928-1972)

Generation No. 9

JOYCE[9] DINSDALE (*EDWIN[8], EDWIN[7], COLLINGWOOD[6], JAMES[5], JOSEPH[4], JOHN[3], JOSEPH[2], THOMAS[1]*) was born July 15, 1928 in Darlington, and died June 1972 in Darlington. She married HARRY HARBURN August 1952 in Darlington. He was born September 21, 1924 in Darlington, and died May 2006 in Darlington.

Child of JOYCE DINSDALE and HARRY HARBURN is:
     i.   ROSLYN HARBURN, b. April 14, 1962.

Pictured right: Joyce on her wedding day in 1952 to Harry Harburn.

Joyce worked as a tailoress at Alexander Workwear in Darlington for some time. Joyce died of cancer aged 42 years.

She had a daughter Roslyn who is now married with two children.

Maureen Dinsdale (1931-2002)

Generation 9

MAUREEN[9] DINSDALE (*EDWIN[8], EDWIN[7], COLLINGWOOD[6], JAMES[5], JOSEPH[4], JOHN[3], JOSEPH[2], THOMAS[1]*) was born February 1931 in Darlington, and died November 2002 in Darlington. She married GRAHAM ALBERT LEONARD October 1954 in Darlington. He died 2002 in Darlington. Occupation: Worked at the Darlington Forge Company prior to marriage, job unknown . GRAHAM ALBERT LEONARD: Served in military (possibly National Service) and was sent out to Malaya in early 1960s. After military service worked at Darlington Forge Company and later other jobs.

Children of MAUREEN DINSDALE and GRAHAM LEONARD are:
  i.   BEVERLEY ANN LEONARD, b. February 1955, Darlington; d. March 1955, Darlington.
  ii. BARRY LEONARD, b. August 1956, Darlington; d. 2007, France.
  iii. ANNETTE LEONARD, b. October 30, 1957, Darlington.
  iv. GILLIAN LEONARD, b. December 20, 1959, Darlington.
  v.   BARBARA E. LEONARD, b. June 9, 1961.
  vi. MARTIN LEONARD, b. August 1962, Darlington.
  vii. GRAHAM EDWIN LEONARD, b. February 1969, Darlington.
  viii. JASON VICTOR LEONARD, b. August 1971, Darlington.
  ix. MICHAEL LEONARD, b. February 1974, Darlington.

Maureen (1931-2002) married Graham Leonard in October 1954 and they had eight surviving children . Prior to marriage, it is thought that Maureen worked at the Darlington Forge Company - though it is unknown in what capacity.

Husband Graham Leonard was doing military service (possibly in the catering core) in the early years of their marriage and was deployed to Malaya. Following the Japanese withdrawal from that area, after their defeat in the Second World War, there was a political vacuum which the Malayan Communist Party tried to fill by engaging in violence in a guerrilla type war against the allied forces, principally the British. The term "war", however, was never used to describe the conflict - as Lloyds of London would have frozen assets/finances if the action had been termed as such, so it was referred to as an "emergency". Well, the "emergency" ended up with some 40,000 British soldiers despatched to quell the communist uprising and by the early-mid 1960s they had succeeded. Graham is thought to have asked wife Maureen to join him out in Malaya but she declined and so he ended his military career and returned to the UK. He worked in various capacities thereafter, including a time at Darlington's biggest employer, the Forge Company.

The couple die within months of each other in 2002.

MIDDLETON GENEALOGY

Descendants of John Middleton

```
1   John Middleton 1703 - 1787
....    +Joan Forster  1710 - 1774
........ 2     John Middleton 1736 - 1811
.............     +Ann Robinson 1740 - 1796
..................3 John Middleton 1762 - 1851
......................... +Elizabeth Middleton 1777 - 1851
........................... 4      William Middleton 1799 - 1859
..............................      +Mary Nattrass - 1837
...............................5 Elizabeth Middleton 1822 -
...............................5 Ann Middleton     1824 -
...............................5 William Middleton 1826 - 1830
...............................5 Mary Ann Middleton 1829 -
...............................5 Margaret Middleton 1833 - 1834
...............................5 William Middleton 1835 -
...........................*2nd Wife of William Middleton:
...............................      +Jane Blackburn 1803 -
.................3 Ann Middleton 1765 -
...........................4       Ann Middleton 1797 - 1837
..............................     +William Binks - 1837
...............................5 Mary Ann Binks     1830 -
...............................5 Mark Binks 1833 - 1888
.....................................+Mary Pattison/Simpson 1831 -
.....................................  6 Mary Binks 1858 -
...............................5 William Binks 1824 -
................. 3 Thomas Middleton 1767 -
................. 3 William Middleton 1770 - 1783
................. 3 Jane Middleton     1773 - 1855
...........................4       Thomas Middleton  1798 -
...............................  +Elizabeth Sickling     - 1825
...............................5 Mary Middleton     1825 - 1825
........................... *2nd Wife of Thomas Middleton:
...............................  +Mary Sickling
...............................  5 Thomas Middleton 1830 -
...............................  +Ellen Harker
...............................      6 John Harker Middleton 1852 - 1922
...............................  +Eliza     1852 -
...............................      7 Clara Middleton 1877 -
...............................7 John William Middleton     1879 -
...............................7 Nellie Middleton 1884 -
...............................7 Christopher Middleton 1886 -
...............................  7 Harry Middleton 1891 -
...............................  7 Mary Middleton 1894 -
...............................  6 Frederick Middleton 1873 -
...............................+Mary Whiting
...............................  7 Neillie Middleton Unknown -
...............................7 Thomas Middleton 1914 -
...............................+Gladys Isabella Grisenthwaite
...............................  8 Frederick Middleton 1935 -
...............................+Sheila
...............................  9 Chris Middleton Unknown -
...............................      +Jenny
...............................  10 Carly Middleton
...............................  10 Leigh Middleton
...............................10 Brett Middleton
...............................9 Lesley Middleton    Unknown -
...............................      +Wayne ?
...............................10 Matthew ?
...............................10 Emma ?
...............................10 Ashley ?
...............................9 Natalie Middleton
...............................      +Max ?
...............................10 Jessica ?
...............................10 Kaylee ?
...............................9 Kimberley Middleton
...............................      +Damian ?
...............................10 Nicholas ?
...............................10 Breenanna ?
```

```
.........................5  Dorothy Middleton 1832 -
.........................5  Charles Middleton 1835 -
.........................5  Jane Middleton      1838 -
.........................5  Elizabeth Middleton 1849 -
.........................4          James Middleton 1813 - 1890
..........................          +Jane 1816 -
.........................5  Mary Middleton      1842 -
.........................5  Jane Middleton      1844 -
.........................5  Sarah Middleton     1846 -
....................+Mr Steele
.........................5  Elizabeth Middleton 1849 -
.........................+Thomas Harland 1849 -
..................................  6  Mary Jane Harland      1870 -
..................................  6  Sara Ann Harland       1871 -
.........................5  John Middleton      1851 - 1923
.........................5  James Middleton     1855 -
............3  Elizabeth Middleton 1776 -
............3  Henry Middleton    1776 -
.................+Mary
........................4          Ann Middleton 1816 -
.........................          +James Fleming 1813 -
............3  Mark Middleton    1780 - 1837
.................+Jane Lockey     1777 - 1861
........................4          Mary Middleton 1806 - 1826
........................4          John Middleton 1808 - 1902
.........................          +Frances Metcalfe  1819 - 1903
.........................5  Thomas Middleton 1839 -
.........................5  John Middleton      1842 - 1861
.........................+Josephina Tornquist     1845 -
..................................  6  Thomas Middleton       1883 -
..................................  6  David Middleton 1885 -
.........................*2nd Wife of John Middleton:
.........................+Jane Tate - 1871
..................................  6  John Robert Middleton 1862 -
.........................5  Robert Middleton 1844 -
.........................5  Elizabeth Middleton 1846 - 1861
.........................5  Jane Metcalf Middleton    1850 - 1877
.........................+John Parker      1847 - 1877
..................................  6  John W Parker 1872 -
.........................+Edith E    1872 -
..................................  6  Tom Parker 1874 - 1929
.........................+Elizabeth Coxon 1876 - 1917
..................................  6  Eliza Jane Parker 1875 - 1931
.........................+George Thomas Green 1875 - 1943
.........................7  John William T Green      1894 - 1969
.........................+Rebecca Abbey 1897 - 1988
.........................8  Rebecca Green      1921 -
.........................8  Olive Green 1923 -
.........................+James Alfred Seago 1922 - 2005
.........................9  Terence Seago 1947 -
.........................9  Carol L Seago 1950 -
.........................9  Stuart Seago  1952 -
.........................9  Stephen J Seago 1955 -
.........................9  Graham G Seago 1956 -
.........................9  Colin Seago 1957 - 1957
.........................8  Thomas Green 1928 -
.........................7  Elizabeth Green 1897 - 1988
.........................+Robert Ross      1897 - 1943
.........................8  Female Ross Unknown -
.........................8  Robert T K Ross 1920 - 1957
.........................+Doris C Melville
.........................8  Kenneth Knowlton Ross 1927 - 1991
.........................+Jean D Bodell
.........................9  Alastair N Ross 1954 -
.........................9  Elspeth F Ross 1960 -
.........................8  Beryl Knowlton Ross 1929 - 2002
.........................+Sydney O Lavelle
.........................9  Janice Lavelle 1964 -
.........................7  Sydney Green      1900 - 1904
.........................7  Edward Green      1905 - 1982
.........................+Sarah Vale
.........................  8  Edward Green 1928 -
.........................8  Ronald Green 1936 -
.........................+Marlene Hall
```

```
..............................................9 David Green   1957 -
..............................................7  Jack Green 1908 -
..............................................7  Evelyn G Green 1910 - 1995
.........................................+Arthur W Dickensen    1912 - 1979
..............................................7 Cissy Green   1913 - 1998
..............................................7 Phyllis Green 1916 - 2002
...............................  6  Annie E Parker 1877 -
..............................................+George W Waite 1877 -
...........................5 Mark Middleton     1853 - 1910
...............................+Christina 1845 - 1898
...............................  6  Frances Middleton        1873 - 1944
..............................................+Michael Watson 1872 -
..............................................7 Mark Watson 1896 -
..............................................7  William Foster Watson    1898 - 1956
..............................................7 Francis Watson        1900 -
..............................................7 Gertrude Elizabeth Watson1902 - 1991
...................................................  +George Arnold Archbold 1899 -
..............................................8  Arnold W Archbold 1925 -
...............................  6  George Middleton        1875 - 1937
..............................................+Gertrude Elizabeth Balderson  1878 - 1916
..............................................7 Christina Middleton 1898 -
...................................  +Herbert Waller
..............................................8  Gertrude Waller 1924 -
..............................................8  Dorothy R Waller   1927 -
..............................................8  Christina Waller 1929 -
..............................................7 Mark Middleton 1905 -
..............................................+Clara Bilbrough 1908 -
..............................................8  Another Middleton
..............................................8  Another Middleton
..............................................8  Another Middleton
...........................5  Mary Middleton     1853 -
...........................5  George Middleton 1858 -
...........................5  Fanny Middleton   1862 - 1888
..............................................+William Coulson 1863 - 1911
...............................  6  Richard Coulson  1888 -
.........................4         Thomas Middleton  1810 - 1876
...............................  +Hannah Ayton 1820 - 1900
...........................5  Mark Middleton     1838 - 1909
..............................................+Jane Middleton nee Fishburn 1874 - 1899
..............................................*2nd Wife of Mark Middleton:
..............................................+[1] Jane Fishburn
..............................................*3rd Wife of Mark Middleton:
..............................................+Elizabeth Fishburn
...............................  6  Elizabeth J Middleton 1860 -
...............................  6  Sarah E Middleton        1868 -
...............................  6  John Stephen Middleton 1869 - 1917
..............................................+Margaret Mary A Oman 1869 -
..............................................7  John Henry Middleton 1902 -
..............................................7  James William Middleton  1908 -
...............................  6  Wilson Middleton        1875 -
...............................  6  Hannah S Middleton 1877 -
...............................  6  Mary Ann Middleton 1880 -
...........................5  John Middleton        1839 - 1849
...........................5  Thomas Middleton 1841 - 1871
..............................................+[1] Jane Fishburn
...............................  6  Margaret Jane Middleton 1865 -
...............................  6  Thomas William Middleton 1870 -
...........................5  William Middleton 1843 - 1913
..............................................+Euphemia Scott 1846 -
...............................  6  William Middleton        1871 -
...............................  6  James Middleton 1872 -
...............................  6  John Thomas Middleton 1874 -
..............................................+Henrietta Brookes        1877 -
..............................................7  Euphemia Middleton 1914 -
..............................................7  Elsie Middleton 1916 -
..............................................7  Muriel Middleton 1919 -
...............................  6  Euphemia Middleton 1877 -
...............................  6  Mark Middleton 1887 -
...........................5  Hannah Middleton 1845 - 1886
..............................................+Christopher Barker 1856 - 1930
...............................  6  John Chapman Middleton 1867 - 1941
..............................................+Marie Bainbridge        1871 - 1941
..............................................7  Amy Middleton 1896 - 1952
..............................................+Ernest Boyes 1886 - 1921
```

.....................................*2nd Husband of Amy Middleton:
....+Jacob Tallentire - 1950
....8 Muriel Tallentire   1925 - 2011
....+Joseph Laycock 1926 - 1991
....9 Linda Laycock 1951 - 1951
....9 Joseph Laycock 1953 - 1996
....9 Barbara Laycock 1955 -
....   +Keith Naisbitt 1946 - 2012
.... 10 Amanda Laycock 1974 -
.... 10 Daniel Naisbitt   1990 -
.... 10 Michael Naisbitt 1991 - 1991
.... 10 Stephen Naisbitt   1993 -
....9 Josephine Laycock 1957 -
....9 John T. Laycock 1960 -
....   +Bridget Wilson
....10 Christopher Laycock 1988 -
....10 Rebecca Laycock 1991 -
....8 Jean M. Tallentire   1931 - 1931
....7 Mabel Middleton 1897 - 1950
....+George Desmond Hutchinson 1897 - 1982
....8 Dorothy Hutchinson 1932 - 2012
....+Clive Tidyman
....9 Caroline S Tidyman 1951 -
....   +Peter W Barron
....10 Tracey Barron 1971 -
....9 Eileen J Tidyman 1953 -
....   +James Griffiths
....10 Darren James Griffiths 1975 -
....10 Penny Griffiths   1978 -
....9 Malcolm Tidyman 1955 - 1955
....9 Brian Tidyman 1958 -
....   +Kaye Hindmarch
....10 Michael Brian Tidyman 1984 -
....9 Gary Tidyman 1960 -
....   +Margaret Leadbitter
....10 Gary Stuart Tidyman 1981 -
....10 Leanne Tidyman 1989 -
....9 Marie D Tidyman 1961 -
....   +Keith J Allcock
....10 Victoria Margaret Allcock   1991 -
....10 Declan Geoffrey Allcock 1994 -
....9 Gillian Tidyman 1962 -
....   +George A Jordan
....10 Aaron Jordan 1990 -
....10 Danielle Jordan   1990 -
....9 Julie Tidyman 1964 -
....8 Barbara Hutchinson 1926 -
....+Alan Beckwith - 2002
....9 Christine Beckwith 1952 -
....   +Anthony Vickers
....10 Samantha Vickers 1979 -
....+Jason Dover
.... 10 John Vickers 1982 -
....10 Paul Vickers 1989 -
....9 Stephen J Beckwith 1954 - 1969
....9 Janet Beckwith 1960 -
....   +Joe Butler
....10 Sheridan Butler   1979 -
....10 Rebecca Butler   Unknown -
....+Kevin Cathrey
....9 John Beckwith 1963 -
....   +Christine Derwent
....10 Luke Beckwith 1994 -
....10 Jack Beckwith   1998 -
....10 Emily Beckwith   2000 -
....9 Gillian Beckwith 1963 -
....   +Yanis Mytakhe
....10 Christina Mytakhe Unknown -
....10 Katarina Mytakhe 1991 -
....10 Andreas Mytakhe 1994 -
....*7 Edith Ann Middleton 1899 - 1972
....   +Edwin Dinsdale 1896 - 1946
.... 8 Elsie Dinsdale 1919 - 1984
....+Harry Blades 1918 - 1999

```
.............................................................9  Malcolm Blades 1947 -
.........................................................................+Pauline Hollis 1961 -
..................................................................10  Jack Malcolm Blades 1995 -
.........................................................9  Moira Blades 1950 -
......................................................................+John Hollis
.............................................................. 10 Laurie Eleanor Hollis 1990 -
...................................................*2nd Husband of Moira Blades:
..............................................................+M. Sanderson
...................................................................10 Dawn Sanderson    1969 -
.......................................................8  Laura Dinsdale 1921 - 1997
...........................................................+Stanley Quentin
.................................................*2nd Husband of Laura Dinsdale:
.............................................................. +John William Proudler 1923 - 2011
.......................................................9  Michael Proudler 1945 -
...................................................................+Diane Hesketh 1948 -
.............................................................10  Jennifer Proudler 1983 -
.......................................................9  Graham John Proudler 1949 -
....................................................................+Karen McLean 1958 -
.....................................................8  Marjorie Eleanor Dinsdale 1923 - 1988
.........................................................+John Marshall Andrews 1918 - 1944
.....................................................9  John Andrews 1941 -
................................................................+Madelaine Baines
.............................................................. 10 Stephanie Andrews 1963 -
.........................................................10  Leslie Andrews    1964 -
.........................................................10  David Andrews    1969 -
.........................................................10  Louise Andrews    1971 -
....................................................*2nd Husband of Marjorie Eleanor Dinsdale:
...............................................................*Frank Peckitt 1923 - 1979
.......................................................9  Pauline Peckitt 1946 -
...................................................................+John Batty
.......................................................... 10 Dean Batty
..............................................................................+.
.....................................................................*2nd Wife of Dean Batty:
.............................................................. +Ruth Calvert
.......................................................8  Maurice Dinsdale    1923 - 1993
.............................................................. +Doreen Holman
.......................................................8  Joyce Dinsdale 1928 - 1972
.........................................................+Harry Harburn    1924 - 2006
.........................................................9  Roslyn Dinsdale 1962 -
...................................................................+Fraser Semple
.............................................................. 10 James Semple 1987 -
.........................................................10  Rebecca Semple    1988 -
.......................................................8  Maureen Dinsdale   1931 - 2002
.........................................................+Graham Albert Leonard 1927 - 2002
.........................................................9  Beverley Leonard 1955 -
.........................................................9  Barry Leonard 1956 - 2007
.........................................................9  Annette Leonard 1957 -
.........................................................9  Gillian Leonard 1959 -
.........................................................9  Barbara E. Leonard 1961 -
.........................................................9  Martin Leonard 1962 -
.........................................................9  Graham Edwin Leonard    1969 -
.........................................................9  Jason Victor Leonard 1971 -
.........................................................9  Michael Leonard 1974 -
...................................................*2nd Husband of Edith Ann Middleton:
.............................................................+Arnold Dinsdale
.................................................7 Mary Middleton 1902 - 1970
.................................................7  Louisa Alice Middleton    1905 - 1958
.....................................................+Edward Seton 1905 -
.................................................8  Audrey Seton 1933 -
.........................................................+Joseph Kenneth Dykes 1934 - 1986
.........................................................9  Pamela Mary Dykes 1956 -
...................................................................+Michael Gibson 1954 -
.........................................................10 Paul Gibson  1984 -
.........................................................9  Barbara Dykes 1957 -
...................................................................+Anthony Steggles  1949 -
.........................................................9  Sandra Dykes 1959 -
...................................................................+Roland Weston 1958 -
.........................................................10  Shane Dykes 1976 -
.........................................................+Julie Bateman    1971 -
.........................................................10  Donna Dykes 1978 -
.........................................................10  Daniel Weston    1981 -
.........................................................+Claire
...................................................*2nd Husband of Sandra Dykes:
.............................................................. +Peter Richards
```

```
...................................................8  Pat Seton 1931 -
...................................................+Raymond Day
...................................................9  Susan E Day  1953 -
...................................................9  Colin R Day   1956 -
...................................................          +Nicola Jordan
...................................7  Wilfred Middleton 1910 - 1910
...................................7  Douglas Raymond Middleton 1918 - 1993
...................................+Doreen
...................................  6  Louisa Alice Middleton 1870 - 1891
...................................  6  Jane Elizabeth Barker 1875 - 1906
...................................+Robert Boyd 1882 -
...................................  6  Hannah Barker 1879 - 1956
...................................+John Binks 1883 -
...................................7  Isabella Binks      1907 -
...................................          +John W Woods
...................................  8 Ivy Woods 1925 -
...................................+Bernard Wilson
...................................   9           Alan Wilson 1950 -
...................................8  Margaret Woods 1926 -
...................................8  Allan E Woods 1936 - 1936
...................................7  John Robert Binks 1910 - 1959
...................................      +Elizabeth B Davison
...................................  8 Malcolm Binks 1941 -
...................................+Christine E De La Mare
...................................9 Andrew Paul Binks 1971 -
...................................      +Suzanne Miller
...................................10 James Leo Binks    2005 -
...................................7  Infant Binks 1905 - 1911
...................................  6  Sarah Barker 1882 - 1896
...................................  6  Christopher Barker      1882 - 1929
...................................+Florence May Mundin 1888 -
...................................7  Florence M Barker 1915 -
...................................7  Christopher J Barker 1920 -
...................................      +Sheila F Eeles
...................................  8 Patricia A Barker   1953 -
...................................+David J Whiting
...................................9 Rebecca Victoria Whiting    1990 -
...................................9 Wayne Malcolm Whiting    1995 -
...................................7  Elizabeth E Barker 1922 -
...................................7  Marjorie Barker 1928 -
...................................  6  Emily Middleton 1885 - 1900
...................................5  Wilson Middleton 1847 - 1849
...................................5  Jane Middleton      1849 - 1871
...................................5  Mary Anne Middleton 1851 -
...................................5  Elizabeth Middleton 1854 -
...................................5  Alice Middleton      1857 - 1941
...................................+Edward Scott     1860 -
...................................6 Ursula H Scott 1886 -
...................................6 Alice M Scott 1888 -
...................................6 James E M Scott 1890 -
...................................6 Robert F Scott 1892 -
...................................6 Florence A Scott 1895 -
...................................6 Edward Scott 1898 -
...................................5 Emily Middleton      1861 -
...................................+John Walker
...................................5 Eliza Middleton      1863 -
...................................  +Alfred Masterman
...................................5 Isabella Middleton 1865 - 1865
...................................4  Sarah Middleton 1813 -
...................................4 William Middleton 1816 - 1853
...................................      +Mary (Caygill or Hirdman) 1815 -
...................................  5 Matthew Middleton       1842 -
...................................  5 Mark Middleton     1844 -
...................................4 Hannah Middleton 1817 -
...................................      +James Sugden 1818 -
...................................5 Mark Sugden 1840 -
...................................5 James Sugden 1843 -
...................................5 William Sugden      1846 -
...................................5 John Sugden 1849 -
...................................5 Thomas Sugden      1850 -
...................................4  Jane Middleton  1821 -
...................................      +Jonathan Tweddell
...................................4  Elizabeth Middleton 1823 -
...................................4  Margaret Middleton 1825 -
```

```
...................3  Chris Middleton Unknown - 1777
........ 2 William Middleton 1738 - 1805
..............+Margaret Calvert
...................3  George Middleton  1765 - 1765
...................3  George Middleton  1766 -
...................3  John Middleton     1766 - 1766
...................3  William Middleton 1767 - 1773
...................3  William Middleton 1773 -
...................3  Christian Middleton 1774 - 1783
...................3  Nancy Middleton   1782 - 1795
...................3  Christian Middleton 1783 - 1836
...........................4  William Middleton 1805 -
...........................4  John Middleton 1811 -
...........................4 William Middleton 1813 -
...........................4 G      eorge Middleton 1816 -
...........................4 Thomas Middleton 1822 -
........ 2  Elizabeth Middleton 1740 -
..............        +Thomas Annall 1744 - 1787
...................3 Thomas Annall 1772 -
.........................+Mary Dobby
...........................4 Robert Annall 1808 - 1868
..................................        +Phoebe Dennison 1808 - 1877
.........................................5  Robert Annall 1840 - 1909
................................................+Rosetta Keith Thornton 1846 - 1906
...............................................  6  Robert William Annall 1871 - 1920
......................................................+Barbara Scott
.......................................................7  Barbara Annall      1904 - 1904
.......................................................7  Doris Annall 1906 -
.............................................................+James Scott
...........................................................    8  Thelma Scott 1936 -
..........................................................8  Christine Scott        1940 -
.......................................................7  Ida Annall 1910 - 1941
.............................................................+Cecil K Smith 1906 - 1978
.......................................................7  Robert William Annall 1911 - 1958
.......................................................7 James Henry Annall 1912 - 1956
.............................................................+Bertha R Barugh
.........................................................    8  Bryon J Annall 1938 - 1976
...................3  William Annall 1774 -
...................3  Isabellah Annall 1775 -
........ 2  Isabella Middleton 1743 -
........ 2  Ann Middleton 1747/48 -
..............+william horner
........ 2  Jane Middleton 1754 -
```

Kate Middleton's Family Tree - Wife of Prince William

And, as to that "other" Middleton line - I'm afraid there is no connection !

Kate Middleton's Family Tree - Wife of Prince William

|

Kate Middleton b. 1982 marries Prince William in 2011

|

Father Michael b. 1949, born Chapel Allerton Nursing Home Leeds marries Carole

|

His father Peter, 1920-2010 (solicitor), marries Adel, Leeds

|

His father Richard Noel Middleton 1878-1951 (solicitor) (Leeds) marries Olive Lupton

|

His father John William Middleton 1839-1887 (solicitor), born St Georges Terrace, Leeds

|

His father William 1807-1884 (solicitor) All Saints Wakefield, died Chapel Allerton Leeds

|

His father John born unknown - joiner and cabinet maker, married 1806 and died Wakefield.

Family Tree for HRH Kate Middleton

SOURCES

Birth Certificate of Hannah Middleton, 1845
Birth Certificate of John Chapman Middleton, 1867
Birth Certificate of Louisa Alice Middleton, 1870
Birth Certificate of Louisa Alice Middleton, 1905
Marriage Certificate of Hannah Middleton, 1876
Marriage Certificate of John Chapman Middleton, 1894
Marriage Certificate of Hannah Barker/John Binks, 1903
Marriage Certificate of Jane Elizabeth Barker/Robert Boyd, 1905
Marriage Certificate of Christopher Barker/Flo Mundin, 1914
Death Certificate of Jane Middleton, 1855
Death Certificate of Jane Middleton, 1861
Death Certificate for Thomas Middleton, 1876
Death Certificate for Hannah Barker, 1886
Death Certificate of Louisa Alice Middleton, 1891
Death Certificate of John Chapman Middleton 1941
Will of Mary Middleton
Probate of Mary Middleton
Family Tree for HRH Kate Middleton

www.ingramcontent.com/pod-product-compliance
Lightning Source LLC
Chambersburg PA
CBHW080309030726
47593CB00009B/2697